JACK THE RIPPER
THE SUSPECTS

THE WHITECHAPEL SOCIETY

PUCK

No. 36. [New Series, No. 14.]   LONDON, SATURDAY, SEPTEMBER 21st, 1889.   Price TWOPENCE.

[Registered as a Newspaper at the G.P.O.]

JACK THE RIPPER.
WHO IS HE?   WHAT IS HE?
WHERE IS HE???

JACK THE RIPPER

THE SUSPECTS

THE WHITECHAPEL SOCIETY

The
History
Press

Frontispiece: JACK THE RIPPER – WHO IS HE? From the front cover of *Puck*, 21 September 1889. (Courtesy of Stewart P. Evans)

First published 2011
Reprinted 2012

The History Press
The Mill, Brimscombe Port
Stroud, Gloucestershire, GL5 2QG
www.thehistorypress.co.uk

British Library Cataloguing in Publication Data.
A catalogue record for this book is available from the British Library.

ISBN 978 0 7524 6286 8

Typesetting and origination by The History Press
Printed in Great Britain

Contents

Acknowledgements

The Whitechapel Society gratefully acknowledges the following for the material and the assistance they have provided: The Bancroft Library; The Bishopsgate Institute; British Library Newspapers; The National Archives; Winchester College Archives; www.casebook.org; www.jtrforums.com; Mark Galloway; Petrina Thompson; Richard Nash; Peter Leyland; Alyn Smith; Richard Clarke; Thomas Toughill; Nicholas Connell; Robert Smith; Roger Palmer and Stewart P. Evans.

A special thank you to our membership for their continued support.

The opinions expressed in this publication are those of the individual authors and do not represent The Whitechapel Society as a whole.

The Usual Suspects

The Jack the Ripper murders, committed in 1888 in London's Whitechapel, are etched into the public psyche. The killings were a criminal benchmark, against which subsequent murderers have been measured. For example, those committed by Peter Sutcliffe – the Yorkshire Ripper, Andrei Chikatilo – the Red Ripper of Rostov and Daniel Rolling – the Gainesville Ripper.

That the Whitechapel Murders have never been solved adds to their fascination. The combination of dingy Victorian streets, blood on the cobblestones, ephemeral clues, fumbling investigators and an unknown mutilator lurking in the shadows, has all the ingredients of a story that continues to captivate the imagination.

Yet, while the crimes remain unsolved, they are not without suspects. In a memorandum penned in 1894, Sir Melville Macnaghten, Head of CID at Scotland Yard, wrote of the murders that, '...many homicidal lunatics were suspected...' He went on to name three of them, two of whom – Druitt and Kosminski – are included in this anthology. Sir Melville would, no doubt, have been astounded to see how the list of suspects has grown over the years.

From a cast of well over a hundred, the names of ten suspects have been selected for inclusion in this book. They include a member of the Royal Family, a barrister, an artist, a brace of hairdressers, a doctor, a quack, a businessman, a fish porter, and a wife murderer. To qualify as a suspect for a criminal offence, there must be reasonable grounds for suspicion, based on knowledge of the person and their background, and what in police circles might be called 'previous', as well as information about conduct and actions.

Common sense suggests that those regarded as suspects in the hunt for the Whitechapel murderer should be measured against a number of investigative criteria. For example, was the suspect known to be in the locality at the time the murders were committed? Was he familiar with the streets and alleyways of the area? Was his appearance such as to create fear or suspicion? How well did he blend into the social background and street scene?

This approach was supported and put on a more professional basis during the centenary year of the murders, in 1988, when American crime profilers applied their knowledge of modern serial killers to the known facts about the Whitechapel Murders. These experts concluded that Jack the Ripper was, almost certainly, male and a person of limited education, intelligence and resources. He probably lived and worked in the locale and would have been normal in appearance and, consequently, not someone who would have invoked suspicion. In profilers` parlance, he was a disorganised serial killer.

Urged on by his paranoid personality, he waited for the right opportunity in order to fulfil his killing instincts. He targeted prostitutes as they were easy prey for the opportunist who readily merged with the local street culture. He was a predator in his own time and place. After each murder, swiftly executed and followed by equally rapid mutilation of his victims, he melted away into the shadows of his comfort zone. Once safely off the streets, likely as not, he was within earshot of the hue and cry breaking out in the neighbourhood at the discovery of a fresh killing.

There is another conceivable measure of the suspect and that is his familiarity with the knife. The hallmark throat-cutting, inflicted on each of the five victims, cannot be denied, nor the swift mutilation and excision of organs which usually followed. A knife was clearly an essential tool of the Ripper's murderous trade. Of our ten chosen suspects, we might suppose that the doctor and the quack knew how to use a scalpel and that the hair-dressers would be familiar with cut-throat razors. On the other hand, of course, anyone might use a knife when compelled to violence.

So, there are some considered criteria against which Ripper suspects might be measured. Readers will judge the suspects chosen by our contributors and form their own opinions.

In some cases, there might be evidence, or arguments, that will be sufficient to keep a particular suspect in the frame. In others, there may be evidence which eliminates a suspect from consideration and, thereby, clears his name. Alternatively, the conclusion reached, after analysing all that is presented about the candidates for the Ripper's mantle, might simply be 'suspect unknown'.

It is the mystery that has sustained the pursuit of Jack the Ripper's identity over such a long period. It is in the natural order of things to want to fill a vacuum and, certainly, there is a void at the heart of the story of the Whitechapel Murders. Perhaps one of our contributors has finally pierced the shadows and directed a spotlight at the true suspect?

Researchers consistently uncover new information, such as the recent revelation about Montague Druitt. The discovery that he was denied membership of the Oxford Union, in 1876, brought new light to bear on what is arguably the most enigmatic remark made about any of the suspects; Macnaghten referred to Druitt as being 'sexually insane'. This indicated that the essence of Druitt's sexual orientation had already been recognised. The case is made that the sources for this contention were his contemporaries at Oxford. These included Evelyn Ruggles-Brise, Private Secretary to the Home Secretary at the time, and Thomas Tuke, owner of the Chiswick Asylum, located close to the spot where Druitt's body was recovered from the River Thames. The likelihood is that Dr Tuke, who later treated Druitt's mother, was the doctor who declared that her son was 'sexually insane'.

We must, of course, keep an open mind, even in the face of apparently compelling arguments. The conduct of research and the recording of history depend on the questing spirit which is not seduced by vapours of the final, definitive word having been pronounced on any subject. We might agree with Francis Bacon when he wrote of suspicion, 'there is nothing makes a man suspect much, more than to know a little.

Robin Odell, 2011

Bibliography

Toughill, T., *The Ripper Code* (The History Press, 2008)
Bacon, F., *Essays: On Suspicion* (1625)

The History of
The Whitechapel Society

THE WHITECHAPEL SOCIETY

Established 1995

Since its establishment by Mark Galloway in 1995, The Whitechapel Society (formerly 'The Cloak and Dagger Club') has fostered the advancement of studies into The Whitechapel Murders and the social history of the Victorian & Edwardian East End.

How it all began...

When Mark Galloway founded the 'Cloak & Dagger Club' back in 1995, he could not have envisaged that it would eventually develop into The Whitechapel Society and the international organisation it has become today. Mark's first real interest in 'Jack' came about when, as a twelve-year-old boy, he came across a book in his local library on the history of the Metropolitan Police, which contained a whole chapter on the Whitechapel Murders and Jack the Ripper. What really interested Mark, like so many of us, was the fact that they never caught the killer.

It was years later that Mark (who is now 'Lifelong Honorary President' of The Whitechapel Society) decided to follow up his early interest and, together with some like-minded people, organised a gathering for a discussion on Jack the Ripper. Gradually the idea consolidated into the notion of a regular club, with a membership list and a bi-monthly meeting – an event that would also include a guest speaker to give a lecture or talk. An ambitious beginning, but the 'Cloak and Dagger Club' was born.

After several successful meetings, it was decided to introduce a membership newsletter; this was the beginning of what would eventually become the highly respected magazine *The Whitechapel Journal*. Society member Paul Daniel was the very first editor and he took the early magazine to a new dimension, producing a first-class publication containing historical articles, book reviews and all the latest research into Jack the Ripper and associated East End of London history.

The Whitechapel Society today...

In 2005, it was decided to rename the club 'The Whitechapel Society' and to ask the question of not who was Jack the Ripper, but why was Jack the Ripper? This simple question allowed us to broaden our research into the Whitechapel Murders of 1888, by looking at a whole spectrum of other, closely related issues. These issues are important because they give us a better understanding of Jack the Ripper, by looking at the world he lived in and what was happening around him. This has resulted in The Whitechapel Society researching and studying workhouses, poverty maps, social conditions, Victorian policing methods and lodging houses and more, resulting in published articles and presentations by, not only Whitechapel Society members, but some of the country's leading experts.

The new direction has allowed The Whitechapel Society to develop, whilst faithfully continuing the tradition started by that small group of enthusiasts over ten years earlier. At the six meetings held each year, members are still blessed with superb presentations and talks from the top experts in the field of Ripperology and Victorian/Edwardian social history. Entry into official meetings remains free to our members and new attendees are always made to feel very welcome indeed! *The Whitechapel Society Journal* has continued to attract many contributors, with articles of every description, from well-known authors to amateurs trying their hands (and often very good ones) for the first time. Now edited and produced by the team of Adrian Morris and Frogg Moody, respectively, members receive six Whitechapel Society Journal magazines per year and are actively encouraged to participate with articles, research, letters and reviews.

In recent years, The Whitechapel Society has diversified, broadened its horizons and explored new, exciting ways of bringing the past to life. Members have been encouraged to participate in a whole host of events, including a photographic history of London's old east end, short story competitions, public exhibitions and 'Question Time' debates. The Whitechapel Society is also proud to be on the steering group of the Tower Hamlets Bancroft Library.

The association between The Whitechapel Society and The History Press, in bringing you this new publication of *Jack the Ripper: The Suspects*, is seen by our organisation as a real achievement and one that takes us to a new level of development. All the contributors are current members of The Whitechapel Society and we are delighted that their meticulous research into each of their given suspects has been rewarded in this book.

Interest in Jack the Ripper, world-wide, remains as strong as ever, and the Society's membership embraces people from all walks of life and from every part of the globe. The Whitechapel Society is open to anyone – all that is required is an interest in Jack the Ripper and his world.

You can become a member of The Whitechapel Society via our website at:

www.whitechapelsociety.com

Our website keeps you up to date with all the latest news involving The Whitechapel Society, Jack the Ripper and historical East End articles.

Go to our official website if you are interested in joining The Whitechapel Society or would like more information.

The Whitechapel Society is the best way to keep in touch with what's happening in the world of 'Ripperology' and the historic East End of London. The Whitechapel Society offers:

Regular Society Meetings
With excellent speakers, conducted in the East End of London, the very heart of the area that we actually study.

The Whitechapel Society: Jack the Ripper London Conference
A two day international conference attracting delegates worldwide.

The Whitechapel Society Journal
The critically acclaimed membership magazine, which features articles, reviews, interviews and much more.

Frogg Moody, 2011

1

The Beatification of Joseph Barnett

Mickey Mayhew

For Monique, who found me; and to my babies, Wolvie and Tiggy

Joseph Barnett holds a rather unique position among Ripper suspects; he's the only partner of one of the victims to be seriously considered as a suspect. But, unlike John Kelly and Catherine Eddowes, for instance, Joseph Barnett and Mary Kelly, as a couple, are also the closest we come to painting a picture of domestic harmony amid all the horror and hyperbole of Whitechapel,in 1888. In fact, given Barnett's proximity to the perpetually elusive Kelly, one wonders why he isn't actually held in higher regard – the privileged person who knew the face that, 120-odd years on, can be reconstructed only from witness statements, given that the photographic evidence is just a forlorn mess. But, when Bruce Paley put Barnett forward as a suspect in his book, *The Simple Truth*, any notions of beatification went by the wayside, as it was suggested that Barnett himself may have been the one responsible for destroying that famous non-face in the first place.

In a nutshell, Paley put forward the hypothesis that Barnett killed the first four canonical victims in order to scare Kelly off the streets, because he disapproved of her lifestyle, and then killed Kelly herself when all these other efforts failed. Her death occurred, according to Paley, after she finally spurned Barnett, a week or so after he'd moved out of the tiny room they shared in Miller's Court, Dorset Street. On the face of it this is possible; in fact, it's fairly plausible. We, as human beings, do crazy things when we're in love, and if the legends of her loveliness live up to the truth about Mary Kelly – no photo other than that of her crime scene is known to exist – maybe we'd understand why Barnett went wild the way he supposedly did. Elevating Barnett to the role of Jack the Ripper may be a touch sensationalist, but there are those willing to settle for his having killed Kelly alone; perhaps in a fit of pique over her return to prostitution. The world of Ripperology remains generous to a tee with the reputations of those it points a finger at.

Joseph Barnett was born and reared within spitting distance of all the murders, at Hairbrain Court, adjacent to the Royal Mint and mere moments from the Tower of London. He was effectively orphaned at an early age, when his father died and his mother seemingly abandoned the family, brought up henceforth by his older brothers. These facts alone are innocuous enough and, indeed, it sometimes seems as if the whole case against him hangs on this loosest of threads. Supposedly, he had a speech impediment – a pronounced stammer or echolalia – that made possible over the years a sort of degeneracy of the personality. For me, the theory falls apart at this first hurdle; which dutifully leads to that dodgy area where innocent men are accused of being the most infamous serial killer in history because of some circumstantial evidence and a soupçon of specially formulated FBI profiling. Whitechapel in 1888 – as the poorest area in London – was full of people who had a lot more to contend with, both physically and mentally, than a stammer. They, as a result, didn't all turn into knife-wielding maniacs. This isn't in any way to do down Barnett's personal experience – of which we know nothing – but Paley's precisely researched pieces on the hardships of East End life, simply don't transfer to putting Barnett on the scene as a serious suspect. In fact, they come across as fleshing out areas otherwise rather bereft of facts. It was a hard world for everybody, full stop. In fact, from all the accounts of Barnett and Kelly's time together, he was anything but the sort of man who went around harbouring a grudge against a cruel and uncaring world. In fact, his whole demeanour and personality positively fly in the face of some of the more fearsome characters and conditions usually conjured up when referring to the Whitechapel of 1888.

Joseph Barnett. (Moody/Morris Collection)

Joseph Barnett met Mary Kelly in Commercial Street on the 8 April – Good Friday – of 1887 and they moved in together the very next day. Whilst this may indeed have been borne of economic necessity for her, for him it certainly seems to have been a case of true love. Barnett was old fashioned by our standards; he worked as a fish porter at Billingsgate market, so she didn't have to ply her trade as a prostitute. The arrangement was suffused with an extra sense of nobility, by virtue of the fact that he was saving her, both body and soul, from the streets with his rather ample wage. Again, rather than conjuring up images of a nefarious, knife-wielding killer, I, for one, am far more put in mind of a well-meaning and rather mild-mannered young man; kind of like a downtrodden, Dickensian Clark Kent, clutching his billycock hat before him and fighting a valiant battle with his b's, as he attempts to mollify her concerns over the constant media coverage of the killings. Without doubt, that is how Joe Barnett ought to be seen; a veritable Superman working his fingers to the bone to give the girl he loved the sort of life she deserved, rather than the sordid reality. Unfortunately, the rather random and indiscriminate realm of Ripperology then rears up, citing him as a possible suspect, simply because of his proximity to Kelly, in the hope of solving a series of murders for which there'll never be any real justice, anyway. It's a sort of slander, swaddled up in an all too human concern for closure. One wonders how diligent these social detectives would be if some snazzy research were to direct an accusing digit at their beloved grandfather or uncle, simply because he visited Bethnal Green occasionally and may, or may not, have worn callipers when he was a child.

Barnett and Kelly moved a couple of times in the early days of their relationship, including a stint on Brick Lane, before settling down in the midst of 'the worst street in London' (Dorset Street), making what home they could in No.13 Miller's Court, a little cul-de-sac that ran off the main thoroughfare. In a room barely big enough to swing a cat – Elizabeth Prater and her kitten, Diddles, residents of the room upstairs, can surely testify to that – they lived in something like domestic bliss for the early part of 1888. By all accounts, Kelly kept off the streets during this period whilst Barnett worked busily in Billingsgate Market, until he had the misfortune to lose his job around the middle of 1888. Bruce Paley put this disastrous turn of events down to theft, one of the few misdemeanours for which a total dismissal was deemed necessary. This could, indeed, have been the case; maybe Mary Kelly was too demanding, even for Barnett's big wage packet, and he had resorted to stealing as a means to keep her in the 'style' to which she had become accustomed. Number 13 Miller's Court may not have been much to look at, but the landlord, John McCarthy, charged a jaw-dropping 4s 6d per week for the 'privilege'. This new set of circumstances put a considerable strain on Barnett and Kelly's somewhat shaky relationship, forcing them to spend much of the day together in their little room, where Barnett could pontificate to his heart's desire on the perils of prostitution, whilst Kelly imbibed increasingly-large amounts of gin in an effort to drown him out. Such a turn of events served only to hasten the end of their somewhat ill-suited relationship, for as much as Joe Barnett may have been her Superman, Mary Kelly was by no means his Lois Lane. If anything, she comes across as a little hard-boiled where Barnett is concerned, with testimony to the effect that she couldn't bear to be in the same room with him. She also saw her former lover, Joe Fleming, from time to time, and summoned a series of female 'friends' to their room to share the meagre space, in what seems to have been a deliberate exercise in driving him out for good. The fact that Barnett continued to give Kelly what little money he had after he'd lost his job, only brightens the hue on his halo as far as I'm concerned. The more cynical might see it as a crude example of someone so unutterably clingy that they can't bear to let go, even when they've been given the boot. The fact was, that from the middle of 1888, Barnett sought almost any work he could in order to keep giving Kelly money, from days spent as a market porter to the occasional stint on the orange markets. Paley hypothesised that the loss of his job and the subsequent lack of money made Kelly's return to the streets imminent, and so Barnett supposedly began his periodic slaughter of prostitutes, in the most ghastly fashion possible, in order to point out to her the perils of such a life.

By all accounts, Kelly was indeed seriously spooked by the spate of killings, begging Barnett to read her the papers after each event. However, even the details of various disembowelments couldn't stop their relationship crumbling, as Barnett's lack of money made their formerly comfortable lifestyle a long-distant memory. Barnett's company seems to have been so intolerable to her that she took in fellow prostitutes – the aforementioned ill-suited 'friends' – to share their room. Perhaps this was partly out of the kindness of her heart, but it also seems a genuine attempt at driving him out. Now that he was earning little or no money he was of no use to her. The final, violent row between them occurred on 30 October, during which Kelly broke several of the windows of their room. This was in consequence of Maria Harvey, a laundress friend of Kelly's, moving into the room Barnett himself moved out, but this didn't deter him from visiting Kelly, on an almost daily basis, and giving her what little money he had. He visited her on the eve of her death, after she'd spent an afternoon mooching around with Maria Harvey. By all accounts, Barnett still loved Kelly so much that he sent his brother Danny to beg her to take him back later that evening, after his own efforts had obviously failed. That she was killed so soon after their split is, of course, the sort of evidence so compelling that it's impossible not to consider him a suspect (but why not his brother Danny; one imagines it will be but a matter of time before a case is launched against him, on the basis of his having tried to reason with Kelly, and then perhaps killing her out of shock over her disregard toward his brother?!). On the other hand, it seems to be just as obvious that without Barnett's protection, Mary Kelly was forced to make her way back onto the streets, where she met her killer. If she'd stayed with him she might have lived, and however meagre Miller's Court might have been, it was still a considerable step up from the succession of common lodging houses or street corners the other canonical victims called home.

Mary Kelly's horrifically mutilated body was found on the morning of the 9 November; it was Barnett who had to identify her, by her eyes and ears alone. He was questioned by police but no case was ever laid against him, and at the time no suspicion seems to have been there either. Barnett was able to come up with a perfectly good alibi, having been ensconced in Buller's lodging house in nearby Bishopsgate. However, the theory maintains, the fact that the door to No.13 Miller's Court was locked and had to be broken down, was proof of Barnett's having stolen the key; which, apparently, Barnett told Inspector Abberline, had gone missing some time back. Barnett then allegedly contradicts himself by saying that they used the broken windows as a means of gaining access to Miller's Court, reaching in and jiggling the lock. However, Barnett had, in fact, moved out on the night when such a means of entrance would first have taken effect. Why then would he have known about the broken window if he left the day the damage was done? My theory is that Kelly hid the key from Barnett some time previously, as insurance in case she ever wanted to lock him out when he became – as he obviously was from time to time – too much for her. Also, it seems plausible that he discovered the alternative means of entrance on one of his subsequent visits, either from Kelly's mouth or one of her friends; gin loosens the lips that way.

I will concede that it could've been Joe Barnett; indeed, when one thinks back on some of that circumstantial evidence, you come to the conclusion that it almost should've been Joe Barnett. And yet it wasn't. After Mary Kelly's death, Barnett moved back into the obscurity

Mary Jane Kelly.
(Moody/Morris
Collection)

from which he came, living for another thirty-eight years, dying in Shadwell with his common-law wife Louisa in 1926. Men who eviscerate innocent women and mutilate them beyond recognition, who take the time to carve the faces of their victims as they lay sprawled in the relative seclusion of Mitre Square, don't retire to a life of quiet sobriety because the object of their affections fell victim to the culmination of their own crazed desires. To the best of my knowledge, Barnett didn't put so much as a foot wrong 'til the day he died. In fact, I'd go so far as to maintain he never actually put a foot wrong in the first place, outside of maybe being dismissed for swiping one too many mackerel for Mary Kelly's supper. Speaking of mackerel, to probe the theory that little bit more, using FBI profiling, Bruce Paley would have us believe that Barnett would '...have sought a job where he could vicariously experience his destructive fantasies, such as a butcher, mortician's helper, medical examiner's assistant, or hospital attendant; Joseph Barnett's job boning and gutting fish provided the necessary atmosphere wherein he could indulge his morbid fantasies.'[1]

One imagines that your average fledgling serial killer would feel very hard done by indeed, if he had to take out all that frustration on a daily catch of cod and kippers. Other research also repudiates some of Paley's suppositions about Barnett and Kelly's relationship, including comments by Philip Sugden in his invaluable *The Complete History of Jack the Ripper*, that '... of Joe Barnett she was genuinely fond.'[2]

The point is, we all want to be the one to catch the Ripper; or do we? If we did, it would probably 'spoil the game' for everyone else and pretty much put the kibosh on what is, in some quarters, a massive media industry, not to mention being the bread and butter of many a tour guide. The mystery hasn't left anyone to avenge, irrespective of any nagging sense of social justice we may experience; and, probably, there's no ghastly grave where the fiend lies for us to go and deface, should we so desire, waving our fists in righteous indignation. Instead, with Joe Barnett, as with so many other suspects, we not only haven't caught the Ripper, but have instead hamstrung ourselves by pointing the finger at him in the first place, armed only with a few petty facts and not much else besides. As Paul Begg has said, Barnett has been singled out purely because he was '...suspected as far as one can tell simply because he was there.'[3]

It sometimes seems that the realm of Ripperology has a quota of people it needs to point the finger at on a regular basis, perhaps to soothe its own collective conscience about being so captivated by all this gruesome stuff to begin with. Like the old adage says, you don't need to blow other people's candles out just to make your own burn brighter. Perhaps Paley, with all his rigorous research, really believed in Barnett's guilt. However, he states the obvious without seeming to realise that many of his facts probably fit half the population of the immediate area, before proceeding to use Barnett's love for Kelly as a stick by which to further beat him: '...not in one of the other theories is a direct and indisputable connection actually proven between the suspect and any of the victims. Nor have any other suspects been reliably placed at or near any of the scenes of the crimes.'[4]

Paley uses frequent bullet points in putting forward his FBI theory. In response, here are a few of my own:

> 1. Barnett had a direct and indisputable connection to Kelly because he loved her, and they were in as normal a relationship as their strained circumstances would allow.

> 2. Barnett could be 'reliably' placed at, or near, the scenes of the crimes because he lived near them, as did 'x' number of other people of considerably more questionable pedigree; in fact one almost envisions a veritable cornucopia of creepy sorts sitting around just waiting to be slandered!

Now, all this isn't to say that I'm painting Joseph Barnett out to be some sort of saint – we are talking about a man who, along with Kelly, was evicted from their room in Little Paternoster Row for being drunk (one imagines eviction in such an area to be quite a feat). But it is one thing to be in your cups occasionally and quite another to have the placard, proclaiming you to be the most prolific serial killer in history, hung around your neck. We ought really to be feting Barnett, not flogging him; were it not for Barnett Mary Kelly would have been even more of an enigma than she already is. Without Barnett we wouldn't have been furnished with many of the facts of her life which he later gave at her inquest and to the papers:

> ...he said she had told him several times that she had been born in Limerick but had been taken when she was quite young to Wales, where her father had been employed at an ironworks in Carmarthenshire. She had also mentioned that she had six brothers and sisters; one of the

brothers was in the army. When she was sixteen she had married a collier named Davis but a year or two later he had been killed in an explosion.[5]

When I first saw the famous picture of Mary Kelly's crime scene I was left speechless, and I think that sums it up about Barnett, especially with regards to his echolalia. Here I am going along with Christopher Scott, whose view of Barnett in regard to such a condition runs thus:

> ...we must, for a moment, ponder the psychological condition in which he would have been at the inquest. He was the focus of press attention in the most notorious case of the day, in the formal, imposing setting of an inquest court, giving intimate and unflattering details about the woman with whom he had lived for a year and a half and who only a few days before had been murdered in an appalling and degrading manner. I think a little hesitancy or verbal stumbling on Barnett's part could be forgiven, and, in my opinion, that is why the coroner commented on the manner in which he had given his evidence, for getting through a harrowing and traumatic experience with a modicum of dignity and lucidity.[6]

Funny how these horrendous events can just take the words right out of our mouths. Proximity to perhaps the most mysterious Ripper victim of all has bred a sort of journalistic jealousy with regards to Joe Barnett. Whilst Bruce Paley's book is a cracking good read for anyone who wants a feel of the flavour of Whitechapel of 1888, along with an impressive amount of research, as far as pointing the finger at Joseph Barnett is concerned – well, it simply isn't true.

Endnotes

1. Paley, B., *Jack the Ripper: The Simple Truth* (Headline Book Publishing, 1996), P. 220
2. Sugden, P., *The Complete History of Jack the Ripper*, (Robinson Publishing Ltd, 1995), p. 308
3. Begg, P., *Jack the Ripper: The Facts* (Robson Books Ltd, 2006), p. 386
4. Paley, B., 'The facts speak for themselves' in Jakubowski, M. ed., *The Complete History of Jack the Ripper* (Robinson, 2008), P. 266
5. Rumbelow, D., *The Complete Jack the Ripper* (Penguin Books, 2004), P.96
6. Scott, C., *Will the real Mary Kelly...?* (Publish and be damned, 2005), P. 128

Bibliography

Begg, P., *Jack the Ripper: The Facts* (Robson Books Ltd, 2006)
Paley, B., *Jack the Ripper: The Simple Truth* (Headline Book Publishing, 1996)
Paley, B., 'The facts speak for themselves' in Jakubowski, M. ed., *The Complete History of Jack the Ripper* (Robinson, 2008)
Rumbelow, D., *The Complete Jack the Ripper* (Penguin Books, 2004)
Scott, C., *Will the real Mary Kelly...?* (Publish and be damned, 2005)
Sugden, P., *The Complete History of Jack the Ripper*, (Robinson Publishing Ltd, 1995)

Mickey Mayhew is a regular contributor to The Whitechapel Society journal, as well as a film and theatre reviewer for a London lifestyle magazine. He is currently studying for his fourth degree – a considerable achievement for someone thrown out of school at thirteen and earmarked for rather poor prospects. He is now preparing a PhD proposal on one of his other big passions, Anne Boleyn.

2

William Henry Bury

Christine Warman

Jack the Ripper was a sexually-motivated serial killer, who terrorised London in the second half of 1888. He eluded both the police and the vigilant public, and left a mystery which continues to fascinate and horrify in equal measure. William Henry Bury was that most commonplace of killers; a man who abused his wife and finally murdered her. He died at the hands of James Berry, the public executioner, on 24 April 1889, in Dundee Prison. William Bury was Jack the Ripper.

William Bury was doomed from birth. He was the fourth child of a young married couple who lived in Stourbridge, in the West Midlands. They were not wealthy, but his father, also called William, was in employment with a fishmonger and they could hope for a happy future. But from the 25 May 1859, when young William first drew breath in this cruel world, the family was heading towards destruction.

William's mother, Mary Jane Bury (née Henley), sank into a state of severe post-natal depression and then, within months, she lost the help and support of her eldest child. Seven-year-old Elizabeth Ann died suddenly at home, after a series of violent epileptic fits. Mary, ill and grieving, was left alone all day with three children under the age of six, while her husband went to work. This involved regular trips to Birmingham with a horse and cart to collect fish. On the 10 April 1850, coming down Muckley's Hill near Halesowen, William Bury Snr had a problem with the horse and jumped down from the cart. He lost control of the animal and it galloped off, crushing his body lengthways under the wheel of the cart. With horrible irony, the papers gave his name as 'James Berry'.

Fate had dealt Mary yet another crushing blow, from which she never recovered. She was soon admitted to Powick Asylum, where she died four years later. The three orphaned children were taken in by Mary Bury's brothers and sisters, and until 1871, William lived with his Uncle Edward's family. When they moved to Ladywood, in Birmingham, they did not take him with them. While it is known that he was educated at the Bluecoate School in Old Swinford, near Stourbridge, it is not known who gave him a home.

It is necessary to record the traumatic events of Bury's early childhood because herein lies the explanation of the man he was to become. His

William Bury standing in the dock. (The *Dundee Advertiser*, 19 March, 1889)

mother was sunken so deeply in her own unhappiness that she could not give him the attention which is vital to the physical and mental health of a growing child. Bereft of love, or subject to abuse, a child cannot develop normally. It is a matter of record that the vast majority of serial killers have had a deprived, or abusive, childhood. The early years of Bury's life would have been terrible. He was 'abandoned' by both parents, and then rejected by his foster family. It is unlikely, but not impossible, that he could remember the horrific death of his sister and the day his mother was told she was a widow. What is certain is that he would have been told about these events, and probably not in the kindest of terms. He would have believed that both his sister and mother were insane, and it is possible that he blamed them for the terrible death of his father. Young children tend to see the loss of a mother as a wilful act of rejection, and Bury would have become very sensitive to further affronts. The anger he felt towards his sister, and mother, led him to regard all women with fear and loathing. Indeed, in adult life he could barely bring himself to be civil to women, under any circumstances. At the same time he longed to bolster his fragile self-esteem by gaining the respect and admiration of other men. However, he was not a homosexual; when he was troubled by sexual desire it was directed towards the female body.

After the almost inevitable murder of his wife in 1889, some information about Bury's life has been preserved in court and police records, and was recorded in contemporary newspaper accounts. People who had known him in Wolverhampton and London came forward to give evidence or speak to journalists. The picture we get is not an attractive one. As a young adult he could read and write well enough to find work as a 'Factor's clerk', according to the 1881 census records for Wolverhampton. He lost his chance for a steady career, with a Mr Bissell, by borrowing money on false pretences, but managed to talk his way into employment with a nearby locksmith. In the short term, Bury could give a good impression, particularly when dealing with other men, but sooner or later, he would always prove to be totally unreliable. In his early twenties, he was already a habitual drunkard. It was said of him at that time, 'In drink he was wholly incapable of controlling himself and when sober he had not the least compunction in deceiving his best friends.' He also had a reputation for irritating his fellow workers with his lies. From those days comes a telling anecdote, which has him being teased by his workmates and breaking a window. This is typical behaviour on the part of someone who was very angry, but also scared. He lacked courage and in later life took to sleeping with a knife under his pillow.

He lost his job with the locksmith, and may have become a vagrant. He was seen scraping a living as a street vendor in Birmingham, but eventually he was drawn in, like so many other desperate people, by the illusory promise of a better life in London. So were some of the Ripper victims. Of the 'Canonical 5', Elizabeth Stride came from Sweden, Catharine Eddowes was born in Wolverhampton and Mary Kelly may have been born in Limerick. Bury arrived in London in the autumn of 1887, and tried to earn a living selling 'cats' meat'. This trade would have required some aptitude with a knife. Being brought up outside the metropolis, he may also have been familiar with the slaughter and dissection of pigs, which so many working people kept in the back yard.

Towards the end of the year, Bury gave up the cats' meat trade and entered into an agreement with one James Martin of No.80 Quickett Street, Bow. Bury was to pay Martin for the use of a horse and cart, and Martin would also sell him supplies of sawdust and silver sand. Bury could keep any profit he made, after paying Martin his dues; this he failed to do. London did not deliver on its promise. Bury was in debt to Martin, yet spent all he had on drink. February 1888 saw him struggling to exist in Bow, but also marks the start of a disquieting series of attacks on women in the capital. Casual, drink-fuelled violence was common enough, but murder was surprisingly rare. Although the common belief is that the Ripper claimed five victims in the 'Autumn of Terror', it is entirely possible that there were more attacks, not all of them fatal.

The murder of Emma Smith, on 3 April, is frequently mentioned in the context of the Ripper killings. Her death bears no similarity to any Ripper attacks, and was most probably the work of a gang which terrorised prostitutes for the sake of their meagre earnings. Of more significance, however, are two knife attacks on women in February and March of 1888. On 25 February, Annie Millward was admitted to hospital with numerous stab wounds to her legs and lower body. No more is known about how and why this happened; she recovered but died a month later of an apparently unrelated condition. This was obviously a sexually motivated attack, though would not have been recognised as such at the time. On 28 March, Ada Wilson was attacked just after midnight by a man with a 'sunburnt' flushed face, who demanded money and almost immediately stabbed her twice in the throat. She was able to scream and he fled.

Meanwhile, Bury had found a way out of his financial difficulties. In addition to trading in sawdust, Martin and a female partner were running a small brothel, and one of the prostitutes attracted Bury's attention. Ellen Elliot, born 24 October 1856, was known to have a modest legacy in the form of shares. She also rented a room in nearby Swaton Street. Bury saw the prospect of wealth and security, but even to achieve this he could hardly bring himself to be pleasant to Ellen, and before their wedding on 2 April, he had already given her at least one beating.

Ellen Bury had drifted through life. She appears to have had a stable upbringing but, as a child, her health had been poor and her education had suffered. She could just about read and write, but with difficulty. She gave birth to an illegitimate child, which later died, and spent some time in the workhouse. It does not seem to have occurred to her to use her nest egg to make her life more comfortable. She became a prostitute and had little contact with her family, other than her married, elder sister Margaret Corney, who was to give evidence at Bury's trial. Ellen had retained enough pride in herself to lodge outside the brothel, and she was fond of her little collection of good jewellery. Having passed her thirtieth birthday, she must have been desperate for the respectability of marriage, even to a man like Bury. Nothing else could explain why she gave in to him. Bury was a little man, morally and physically. He stood 5ft 3½ ins tall, and weighed under ten stone. He had dark hair and a face, that with drink, or emotion, became flushed. Oddly enough, newspaper reports from his trial describe him variously as 'decent looking' but also 'insignificant' and even 'feeble-minded', and with having a Jewish look about him. In his personal conduct, he seems to have clung to just one shred of self-control in that he kept the Sabbath by not drinking on a Sunday.

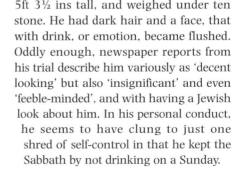

Portrait of Ellen and William Bury.
(*Midland Weekly News*, 16 February, 1889)

For mos, of the short period of their marriage, Bury treated Ellen abominably. He beat her, took all her money from her and, by May, he had given her a sexually transmitted disease. More to the point, within days of the wedding, Mrs Haynes, the couple's landlady at Swaton Road, caught him holding a knife to Ellen's throat. Bury managed to force Ellen to sell some of her shares; with which he bought a horse and cart of his own, in order to trade in sawdust, but apparently he did more drinking than actual work. He was also under the necessity of finding other lodgings, because his behaviour had become so intolerable that Mrs Haynes told the couple to leave. They lodged first in Blackthorn Road and then in nearby Spanby Road, close to the stable where the horse was kept.

Bury was still finding life difficult. Other people were able to notice and criticise his conduct, and he found he was forced into a parody of domestic life, when his every instinct revolted against being in the company of a women, except to relieve a sexual need. He was to find a way to get satisfaction without even a semblance of emotional involvement.

Martha Tabram, or Turner, is gaining acceptance as a Ripper victim. She was a prostitute and after a busy evening with some soldiers, she met with one last client. She was found dead of multiple stab wounds in the small hours of 7 August. The intent was plainly to kill, and her murderer had begun to explore a little further by inflicting an 'incised' wound in the region of her private parts. This wound bled out and probably left the killer stained with blood.

Martha was known to suffer 'rum fits', from alcohol withdrawal. The most likely scenario is that she led her killer to a quiet spot to have intercourse, but then lost consciousness. Bury was confronted, yet again, by total rejection as Martha became oblivious to his presence. He stabbed her in anger – he always had a knife about his person – and then was thrilled to discover that he was in total control and in no danger of further affronts to his self-esteem.

Later, that August, Bury felt the need for a holiday, and took Ellen to Wolverhampton. He was looking forward to showing his former workmates that he had made good. He flashed 'his' money around, boasted of Ellen's prospects, and graciously permitted her to buy some more jewellery. It was all a sham. Back in London, he continued drinking heavily, and by the end of the month the work of Jack the Ripper had begun in earnest.

He found ways to refine the process. First he strangled his victim, either by hand or with a ligature. Whether or not this was instantly fatal, the resulting loss in blood pressure would reduce arterial spray when the throat was cut across. When this was done, the killer was free to open the body to mutilate, remove, and even assimilate what he believed to be the significant sexual organs. In his mean-spirited way, he also rummaged through his victims' pockets and may have taken a few souvenirs. He did not think of himself as Jack the Ripper; that name was bestowed upon him by a journalist. The killer wrote no letters, scribbled no graffiti, and did his best to avoid being noticed.

He usually hunted towards the end of the week, but he never struck during his Sabbath time of abstemiousness; he was cautious. He left his den to hunt in Whitechapel, and his victims were women who were peculiarly vulnerable. He took Polly Nichols on 31 August, Annie Chapman on the 8 September, and both Elizabeth Stride and Catherine Eddowes on 30 September. On 9 November, Mary Kelly let him into her small room in Miller's Court. Without fear of being interrupted, he was able to take her body apart. He took out the heart, a powerfully symbolic act. This organ was never found and he probably ate it. As well as destroying Mary's body, he burnt some of her clothes in the fireplace. Then he managed to slip away unnoticed. One of the biggest problems in identifying the Ripper lies in the variety of eye-witness testimony about probable suspects. Bury was small and rather nondescript; if seen, he left no strong impression. He could be any or none of the sightings.

After his climactic experience with Mary Kelly, he was emotionally drained and also increasingly fearful. The entire nation was obsessed with the Ripper and the police were at their most vigilant. The press had also reported further alleged sightings, and Bury thought he could be identified. He may have made a half-hearted attempt to take a victim in Poplar, when Catherine Mylett was choked to death in late December, but by January he decided he had to leave London. He had nothing left to lose; his business had gone and there was very little left of Ellen's money.

With a crudely forged letter, apparently offering the pair of them employment, he tricked Ellen into accompanying him to Dundee. The work never materialised, but she was now unable to leave him even if she tried. He was, however, at least presenting the appearance of a dutiful husband and the couple were seen well dressed and apparently happy. They arrived on 20 January and took lodgings with a Mrs Robinson, at 8s a week, but with a flash of his old hostility to women, he alarmed her by trying to beat her down to 6s. He then gained access to a derelict basement at No.113 Princes Street, by taking the keys in order to view it – and there Ellen's life was soon to end.

For a week or so, Bury was to spend the last of their savings trying, as ever, to make a big impression in the local pubs. He bought rounds of drinks, and a naïve young man called Walker found him fascinating company. Ellen felt out of place so far from London and did not mix much with her new neighbours, though she and her husband did meet with a couple called Smith. When she was alone with them, she confided in them that her husband had fallen into bad company in London and was in the habit of stopping out at night. When he came back, the talk turned to Whitechapel and Ellen said, 'Oh, Jack the Ripper is quiet now.' Women who suspect the worst will try to hide the thought, even from themselves, but Bury began to fear that his secret would be revealed.

Ellen was never seen alive again after Monday 5 February; she may have died in the early hours of Tuesday. Bury went out and about, but his door was left locked and the blinds drawn. He went on drinking, but also went as a spectator to the Dundee Magistrates' Court and watched the proceedings with fascination. At noon, on Sunday 10 February, he visited his new friend Walker at home, and they looked over the *People's Journal* together. Bury read, with interest, an account of a woman committing suicide with a rope around her neck, but Walker alarmed him by asking if there was anything about Jack the Ripper, 'you that knows the place.' Bury went out, pretending Ellen was cooking a good dinner, but he was soon back and the two men went to look at the ships in the harbour. But Bury did not plan to sail away. All he could think of now was a way to avoid being blamed for his wife's death.

That evening, Bury went to the Central Police Station and claimed that his wife had strangled herself, and being both angry and afraid that he would be accused of being a 'Jack the Ripper', he had attempted to cut her up and hide her in a box. Detectives Lamb and Campbell went to the basement and found a scene of chaos. The remains of Ellen Bury were discovered – packed tightly into a wooden crate. She had been strangled, but there were also cuts to her lower abdomen and part of her intestines protruded. In order to force her into the crate, one of her legs had been broken. A cord lay on the floor, and on a windowsill, the officers found a knife with blood and hair upon it. Clothes and other items had been burnt in the fireplace. In another wooden box the police found male clothing and cheap jewellery, including two finger rings (Annie Chapman had been robbed of two brass rings). Ellen's good jewellery was now in Bury's pockets.

What did Ellen know? In the back stairway leading to the ash pit, where only she would go, the barely literate woman had chalked two messages which were to cause a local sensation:

Jack Ripper is at the back of this door

Jack Ripper is in this seller

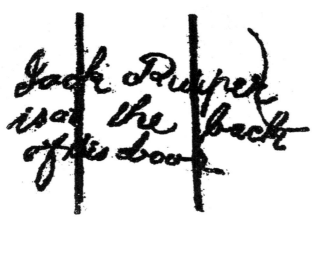

The two chalked messages which caused a local sensation. *(Dundee Advertiser,* 1889)

Bury could, surely, not have known what she had done but, if he thought Ellen suspected that he was the Ripper, he may have begun to fear that she would do more than merely make sly remarks to people like the Smiths. This would have given him a strong motive for silencing her, but it is just as likely that they fell out about money, when he threatened to take her last asset – her cherished jewellery. What is less likely is that he succumbed to his compulsions. After ten months of marriage, she simply would not stimulate his perverse appetite, besides which, the selection and hunting down of a victim were probably important to him. Nevertheless, once he had strangled Ellen and stripped off her clothes, the sight of her dead, naked body revived his desires and he was compelled to mutilate her remains.

Rather to Bury's surprise, the police did not believe his tale of suicide, and he was quickly put on trial for murder. The case opened at Dundee on 28 March; George, Lord Young was on the bench. Even without the suspicion that Bury was the Ripper, the proceedings have some points of interest. Bury was ably defended by a young advocate, William Hay, who probed every weak spot in the medical evidence, in order to keep alive the possibility that Ellen had killed herself. Meanwhile the prosecution irritated the jurors by making a mockery of a Dr Lennox, whose evidence supported the defence case. The jury then astounded the judge by giving a rather muddle-headed verdict. This was 'guilty' but with a recommendation of mercy, in view of conflicting medical evidence. They were sent back to come to a more sensible decision, and this time they simply said 'guilty'. Bury eventually admitted to killing Ellen, but claimed in a letter, to the Revd E.J. Gough, that he was driven to it by Ellen's conduct. To the last, Bury was trying to make a good impression.

Hay did his best to appeal, on the grounds of his client's insanity, but this was not allowed, and the date of Bury's execution was set for 24 April 1889. The Scottish press, and some American papers, took him seriously as a Ripper suspect, and police officers from London did come up to Dundee to take a look at Bury, but higher ranks in the capital did not take the matter very seriously; Bury simply did not fit in with their preconceived ideas of the Whitechapel killer.

One man was convinced of Bury's guilt, and that man was the one person closest to him at the end: James Berry, public executioner. He reported that Bury said to him, with some emphasis, 'I suppose you think you are clever because you are to hang me, but because you are to hang me you will not get anything out of me.' James Berry also claimed, in his memoirs, that quiet men in suits told him, privately, that London would no longer be troubled by Jack the Ripper; but of course, Berry did have a book to sell.

So, why did William Henry Bury drop out of sight as a suspect? Bury was simply too dull. He was a wretched little man, but this is precisely why he is a very good suspect today. He conforms to the typical profile of the sexual serial killer as an embittered loner, unable to gain the respect he craves. More to the point, Bury was loose at night, at the time when the Ripper struck in London. While the death of Ellen Bury has eerie similarities to known Ripper Murders, although in 1889 these were not recognised. She was strangled, then mutilated post-mortem, and her killer used fire to dispose of some of her belongings. Ellen believed she was married to Jack the Ripper, and this shy, insecure little woman was uniquely, and tragically, in a position to recognise him for what he was.

Bibliography

Beadle, W., *Jack the Ripper: Anatomy of a Myth* (Wat Tyler Books, 1995)
Beadle, W., *Jack the Ripper Unmasked* (John Blake Publishing, 2009)
Macpherson, E., *The Trial of Jack the Ripper* (Mainstream Publishing, 2005)

Christine Warman was born in Birmingham. She spent most of her working life in the retail trade, but is now retired and lives with her husband near Whitby. Christine is a member of Mensa. Her magpie tendency to pick up information has led to a couple of (brief) appearances on Mastermind. Christine is a member of the Whitechapel 1888 Society.

3

Severin Klosowski, alias George Chapman

Sue Parry

My candidate for Jack the Ripper is Severin Klosowski, also known as George Chapman, a convicted killer who was hung in 1903, following the murders of three women. Indeed, it was said that Frederick George Abberline, a senior police officer on the 1888 case, declared at the time of the Chapman's arrest, 'You've got the Ripper at last.'

Severin Antonio Klosowski was born in Poland on 14 December, 1865, to Antonio, a carpenter, aged thirty, and his wife Emilie aged twenty-nine. Between the ages of eight and fifteen, he attended a rural primary school and a school report described his conduct as 'very good'. On leaving school, he was apprenticed for a period of four and a half years to a surgeon. He was described as 'diligent' and of 'exemplary conduct', studying with 'zeal' the science of surgery whilst 'under doctor's instructions rendered very skilful assistance to patients.' His name was entered in a registry of surgical pupils in 1885, and from October 1885 to January 1886, he studied at the Hospital of Praga in Warsaw – again his conduct was described as good. Klosowski appears to have achieved the status of Junior Surgeon, by December 1886, and paid his fees to the Treasury of the Warsaw Society of Assistant Surgeons up until March 1887.[1] He then left Warsaw and came to London, but opinion varies as to the exact date of the emigration. On his arrival in London he worked as a hairdresser for Abraham Radin, in West India Dock Road. He remained in Mr Radin's employ for about five months.[2] Klosowski then appears to move on, working as a self-employed hairdresser in Cable Street. In 1890 he worked first as an assistant,and then as the proprietor of a barbers in the basement below the White Hart public house, on the corner of Whitechapel High Street and George Yard (now Gunthorpe Street).

In the later part of 1889, Klosowski met Lucy Baderski at a Polish club in Clerkenwell.[3]After a brief courtship, of only four or five weeks, they were married on 29 October 1889. Initially they lived together at No.126 Cable Street.[4]A son, Wladyslaw, was born on 6 September 1890, but died on 3 March 1891. At the time of their son's birth, the couple were living at No.89 High Street, Whitechapel. However, by the time of the infant's death, they had moved to No.2 Tewkesbury Buildings, Whitechapel[5], and they were still there when the census was taken on 5 April 1891. The couple then emigrated to the United States[6] and settled in New Jersey. However, Klosowski was acting violently towards his wife and, in February 1892, Lucy returned to the UK and gave birth to a girl, Cecilia, on 15 May.[7]

Klosowski returned from the US shortly after the birth of Cecilia and was re-united with his wife.[8] It was Klosowski who registered the baby's birth, on 20 June, and at that time the family were residing at No.26 Scarborough Street, Whitechapel.[9] However, by November 1893, Klosowski was living with a woman named Annie Chapman (no connection to the Ripper victim). They lived together as Mr & Mrs Klosowski in West Green Road, Tottenham, but Annie left him about a year later. She was to claim later that she had a child by him.[10] It seems that, from this point, Klosowski adopted the name George Chapman, so from here on I will refer to him as that.

In 1895, Chapman met a Mrs Mary Isabella Spink (neé Renton) in Leytonstone. Mrs Spink's husband, Shadrach, had deserted her, taking their son (also named Shadrach) in 1890; shortly after the desertion, Mrs Spink gave birth to a second son, William.[11] By October 1895, the couple were telling people that they were married, though both were still married to others, and no record exists of a marriage ceremony.[12] Mrs Spink had been left £500-600, by her grandfather,[13] and it was not long before this money found its way into Chapman's pockets. In early 1897, he used it to buy the lease on a small barber's shop in George Street, Hastings.[14] The family of three – Mrs Spink, Chapman and young William – lived in Hastings and by May of that year, Mrs Spink was frequently vomiting. It is likely that Chapman was also subjecting her to physical violence. They left Hastings in September 1897, and Chapman, making a career change, became the licensee of the Prince of Wales Pub in St Bartholomew Square, just off the City Road in London. Mrs Spink's health rapidly deteriorated; she had lost a good deal of weight and suffered frequent bouts of sickness and diarrhoea. A Dr J.F. Rodgers was in attendance, and on Christmas Day 1897, this unfortunate woman died an agonizing death, aged forty-one years. Dr Rodgers gave the cause of death as phthisis (tuberculosis).[15]

Chapman played the grieving husband, but one month later, he applied for young William to be taken into a Dr Barnardo's Home. He was not admitted to the home, but at a later date he had him taken into the Shoreditch Workhouse.[16]

By Easter 1898, Chapman had appointed a new barmaid at the Prince of Wales: Elizabeth (Bessie) Taylor. They soon entered into a relationship and, just like the previous Mr & Mrs Chapman, they were telling people that they were married. Around the middle of 1898, Chapman bought The Grapes public house in Bishops Stortford.[17] During their brief stay there, Bessie became ill and spent sometime in the hospital in the town. She was suffering abuse at the hands of Chapman and by March, 1899, the couple had sold The Grapes and moved on to another pub, The Monument Tavern, No.135 Union Street in Southwark. Just like her predecessor, Bessie's health was deteriorating. She was suffering from exhaustion and pains in her stomach; she consulted a Dr James Morris Stoker several times at his surgery. However, her condition worsened; she was now suffering from vomiting and diarrhoea and complained of a burning sensation in her throat. Dr Stoker was in attendance almost daily, from 1 January 1901, and asked three other doctors to give their opinions: 'womb trouble', cancer, and 'a severe form of hysteria' were all suggested! Bessie died on 13 February 1901; she was thirty-six years old. On the death certificate, Dr Stoker gave the cause of death as 'intestinal obstruction, vomiting and exhaustion.'[18] This time Chapman displayed a callous indifference to his 'wife's' death. Interestingly, in the April 1901 census, Chapman is recorded as the publican of The Monument public house; he described his marital status as 'single' and place of birth as 'United States'.

In August 1901, Chapman employed eighteen-year-old Maud Marsh. Again, within a short period of time they were telling people that they were married; having told Maud's parents that Chapman was a widower.[19] In December 1901, the couple moved to a nearby pub, The Crown, following a serious fire in which The Monument burnt down. In June 1902, a young barmaid, Florence Rayner, was employed at The Crown. Within a fortnight of Florence's arrival, Chapman was making advances towards her and suggested that they go to America together; Florence would go first, Chapman would sell his business and then follow her. When Florence protested that he had a wife, Chapman replied, 'If I give her that [snapping his fingers], she would be no more Mrs Chapman.' Florence left The Crown after three or four weeks.[20]

The relationship between Chapman and Maud had become violent, and Maud confided in her sister Louisa that Chapman 'had beaten her more than once, taking hold of her hair and banging her head.'[21] Just like the two previous 'Mrs Chapman's' Maud became ill, suffering from severe vomiting, diarrhoea and abdominal pains. She was admitted to Guys Hospital on 28 July, 1902, where her illness confused her doctors; she remained there until 20 August.[22] However, she improved during her time in hospital and returned to The Crown, but then her symptoms rapidly returned. On 10 October she too consulted Dr Stoker.[23] Maud's mother, Eliza, arrived at the pub on 20 October to nurse her daughter[24] and Maud's father, Robert, very concerned for his daughter's health, arranged for his own doctor, Dr Grapel, of No.282 London Road, Croydon, to visit Maud at The Crown, on 21 October.[25] Dr Grapel was initially baffled by Maud's condition, but on his way back to Croydon, he came to the conclusion that this could well be a case of repeated arsenic poisonings, but he was reluctant to communicate this to Dr Stoker as he had no proof. He fully intended to get in touch with Dr Stoker the following day, but before he could do so, Mr Marsh showed him a telegram he had received, telling him of his daughter's very sudden and agonising death, at 12.30 p.m. that day, 22 October 1902. On hearing this distressing news, Dr Grapel sent Dr Stoker a telegram, in which he conveyed his suspicions.[26] The following day at The Crown, Mrs Marsh, her daughter Alice, and Maud's aunt were having tea with Chapman, unaware of the storm gathering over his head. Not letting the grass grow under his feet, Chapman said to Alice, 'There is a chance for you as barmaid now. Will you come?' Naively she replied, 'No thanks, London does not suit me.'[27]

Shaken by Dr Grapel's telegram, Dr Stoker refused to sign a death certificate and arranged for tests to be carried out on Maud's organs. The results showed that both arsenic and antimony, were present in the victim's remains.[28] On 25 October, Dr Stoker contacted the police, and Detective Inspector George Godley and Inspector William Kemp went to The Crown. Chapman was arrested and that night was charged with the murder of Maud Marsh.[29] It was while the police searched the pub that they found paperwork which clearly showed that George Chapman and Severin Klosowski, despite his protestations,[30] were one and the same man.[31]

The bodies of Mrs Spink and Bessie Taylor were exhumed and both contained considerable amounts of antimony. On 31 December Chapman was charged in the name of Severin Klosowski with the murders of Mary Spink and Bessie Taylor.

On 11 February 1903, Chapman was committed for trial at the Central Criminal Court; the trial commenced on 16 March. Sir Edward Carson KC, the Solicitor General, was the prosecuting counsel; Mr Elliott defended Chapman and the judge was Mr Justice Grantham. Chapman pleaded 'Not guilty' to all three counts of murder. However, the jury were then instructed to try for the case of the murder of Maud Marsh. Forty-three witnesses gave evidence for the prosecution, including members of all his victims' families, the family of Lucy Baderski, Annie Chapman, Drs Grapel and Stoker, and of course Detective Inspector Godley and Inspector Kemp.[32]

One interesting witness was William Davidson, a chemist from Hastings who testified that on 3 April 1897, George Chapman purchased one ounce of tartar-emetic.[33] Sir Edward Carson had explained to the jury, earlier, that the main ingredient of tartar-emetic was the irritant poison antimony. Tartar-emetic is a white powder which is easily soluble in water and causes vomiting, diarrhoea, abdominal pain, weight loss and often a burning sensation in the throat. One ounce of tartar-emetic would have contained at least 146 grains of antimony. The ingestion of two grains can be fatal, while ten to twelve grains would undoubtedly produce death.[34] Mrs Spink's body contained nearly four grains of antimony, Bessie Taylor's contained over twenty-nine and Maud Marsh's body contained just over twenty grains.[35] The fact that

George Chapman in the dock. (*Thomson's Weekly News*, 21 June, 1930)

Mrs Spink's body had been in the ground for nearly five years would account for why so little antimony was found, but, in the words of prosecuting counsel, the other two bodies were 'soaked' in the poison.

Another significant witness was Jessie Toon, who had been employed by Chapman to nurse Maud Marsh for the last twelve days of her life. She testified that Chapman had administered a liquid to Maud on a number of occasions, which he had prepared, always washing the container himself. Towards the end of Maud's life, Chapman supplied all Maud's drinking water in a jug and prepared all her food. Chapman told the nurse that it was a mixture of beef tea, egg and milk and he administered it to Maud through a syringe and rubber tube. Not surprisingly, Maud would vomit these preparations back and be in considerable pain. Again, Chapman washed all the feeding apparatus himself. She confirmed that Chapman was becoming very nervous about Mrs Marsh's presence, advising Toon to be careful what she said to Maud's mother and to report to him anything that Mrs Marsh said. Toon also described how, on the day of Maud's death, Chapman gave the victim some brandy and water. On taking a sip Maud cried out, so Toon tasted it herself; she said it tasted as though there was a 'foreign substance' in it. She described how this liquid had burnt her lips and she had had to wash her mouth out.

Mrs Marsh also testified that after drinking some brandy and soda, which had been given by Chapman, as she sat at her daughter's bedside, she too was seized with violent stomach pains. Jessie Toon said that Chapman appeared to find this funny and told her, laughing, that 'The old mother is bad now.'[36]

In Mr Justice Grantham's summing up, he launched a scathing attack on Dr Rogers' competence, berated the three doctors called to give second opinions in the case of Bessie Taylor and expressed exasperation at the conduct of Dr Stoker. He paid tribute to Mr and Mrs Marsh, Maud's parents, and said that if it had not been for their actions, the cause of the death of their daughter would not have been established and there could well have been more victims. Dr Grapel faired only a little better in this onslaught, when the judge said, '...this is the first time in all these long years that any intelligence has been brought in.' However, he quite rightly attacked him for not communicating his (correct) diagnosis at once, or returning to the sickbed when there was not a moment to lose, and suggested that his visit had prompted Chapman to administer one more large and fatal dose. The judge was in his stride now and continued his attack on the doctors at Guys Hospital who failed to discover the cause of Maud's illness, and failed to draw any conclusions when her condition improved whilst in the hospital, but deteriorated when she returned to The Crown.[37] After reviewing the four days of evidence presented before the court, the judge asked the jury to retire and consider their verdict in the case of the murder of Maud Marsh. The jury retired at 5 p.m. and in ten minutes had returned with a verdict of 'guilty'.[38]

After his conviction, Chapman was removed to Wandsworth Prison where he was hung, still proclaiming his innocence, on the morning of 7 April 1903. He was thirty-eight years old.

After Chapman's conviction, the police reviewed the Jack the Ripper Murders of 1888. Certainly Abberline, from his retirement in Bournemouth, felt strongly that Chapman and the Ripper could be one and the same man and expressed his thoughts in an interview with the *Pall Mall Gazette*. So other than being a convicted killer, what evidence do we have?

The exact date of Chapman's arrival in London is not known. It has to be after March 1887 (his last payment to the Treasury of the Warsaw Society of Assistant Surgeons). At Chapman's trial, Mrs Radin (wife of Abraham Radin) says that Klosowski (Chapman) worked for her husband for five months and during that time 'her baby was ill and he helped her in the treatment of it.'[39] That baby was Solomon Radin, born 26 May 1887.[40] To describe a child as a 'baby', it is reasonable to assume that it is under one year old, giving a latest date of arrival as May 1888. We can now say, with confidence, that Chapman was in the East End of London at the time of the Whitechapel Murders.

Chapman's frequent change of job, and address, make it difficult to decide where he was living in the Autumn of 1888. From the evidence given during his trial and his marriage certificate of 1889, it seems his most likely address was No.126 Cable Street, St George's-in-the-East. This is well within striking distance of all the Ripper murder sites.

The date when Chapman and Lucy Baderski departed for America is hard to pin down. Their baby son had died in March 1891, and they appear on the census of the 5 April. At Chapman's trial, Lucy Baderski's sister testified that Lucy returned from America alone in February 1891, and another child was born on 12 May.[41] This is, of course, at odds with the April 1891 census, which clearly showed that Chapman was present in the UK, and the birth certificate of that second child clearly shows that she was born on 15 May 1892.[42] Therefore, given that this evidence was given some ten years later, I believe that Lucy's sister was mistaken about the year and that Lucy's return was indeed in February 1892. However, she did say that Chapman returned from America when the baby was two weeks

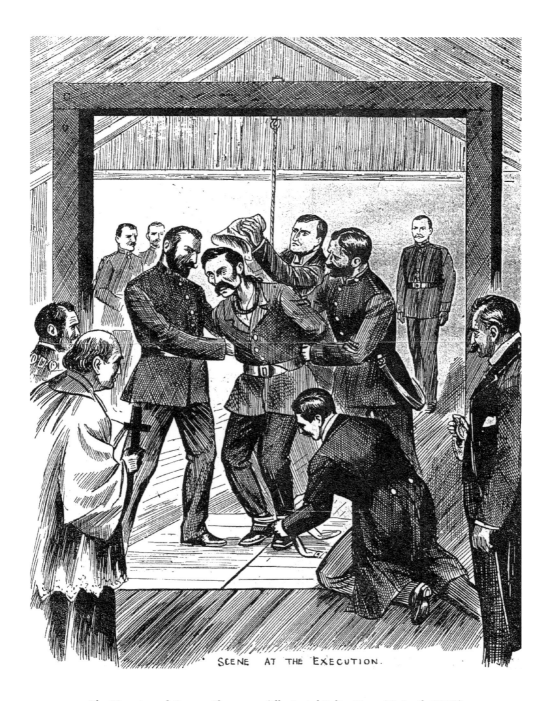

SCENE AT THE EXECUTION.

The Hanging of George Chapman. (*Illustrated Police News*, 18 April, 1903)

old, therefore putting his return at the end of May 1892, which is consistent with him registering the baby's birth himself on 20 June. On cross-examination, she said that the couple had departed for America at 'Whitsuntide'.[43] Therefore, I believe that Chapman was in America from late May/early June 1891 to late May 1892. A New York prostitute, Carrie Brown, was found murdered and mutilated in a Ripper-style killing, outside the run-down East River Hotel on 24 April 1891. An Algerian was convicted of her murder and sentenced to life imprisonment. However, this was widely believed to be an unsound conviction and he was released after eleven years. Many have said that this murder could have been the work of George Chapman, but the dates I have outlined above make this unlikely, though not out of the question. However, it would have meant that Chapman only had between 5 (date of the census) and 24 April to depart the UK, sail to New York, select a victim and carry out the murder – so I am inclined to rule out Carrie Brown as being a victim of George Chapman.

However, as well as Chapman being in the locale at the time of the murders of the 'Canonical 5', the murder of Martha Tabram (7 August 1888) could well have occurred after Chapman's arrival in London; and certainly the murders of Annie Farmer (20 November 1888), Rose Mylett (20 December 1888), Elizabeth Jackson (June 1889), Alice Mackenzie (17 July 1889), the Pinchin Street torso (September 1889) and Frances Coles (13 February 1891) occurred when Chapman was in the East End. No further victims have been suggested to have occurred after February 1891, which fits nicely with Chapman's departure for New York around May/June 1891.

Chapman's known murderous activities started around May 1897. If Francis Coles was a Chapman victim, then there was an interval of just over six years. This is not without precedent; Peter Sutcliffe, the Yorkshire Ripper, had an interval of five years and ten months between his first two attacks.

The description given by George Hutchinson of the man seen with Mary Jane Kelly was: 5ft 6in tall, aged around thirty-four, with a dark complexion and a moustache curled at the end. Other than the age, this fits Chapman well. At the time of the Kelly murder, Chapman would have been twenty-three. However, the photograph of Chapman with Bessie Taylor and another with Maud Marsh, when Chapman would have been in his mid-thirties, show a much older looking man. At his trial, Lucy Baderski's brother and sister both said that Chapman's appearance had changed very little since the first time they had met him.

It was thought that Jack the Ripper had medical knowledge, particularly with reference to the case of Catherine Eddowes. Chapman undoubtedly had the medical knowledge to remove this poor woman's kidney and uterus.

All of this is, of course, circumstantial evidence. Is there an argument against Chapman being Jack the Ripper? If Chapman were the Whitechapel murderer, he would have changed from murdering prostitutes, who were probably strangers to him, to murdering women from an entirely 'respectable' class who were known – indeed were close – to him. He would have changed from cutting throats and savagely quick and highly violent deaths – each one more vicious than the last – to the slow, drip-drip, long, drawn-out deaths that antimony produces. However, Abberline addressed that very point in the *Pall Mall Gazette* interview, when he said, '...incentive changes, but fiendishness is not eradicated. The victims too, you will notice, continue to be women; but they were of different classes, and obviously call for different methods of despatch.' John Douglas, of the Behavioural Science Unit of the FBI, says on his website that serial murders generally surface in their mid to late twenties (Chapman would have been nearly twenty-four during the Autumn of Terror). He would argue that Chapman did not start killing when he was in his mid-thirties; it is likely he would have started about ten years earlier. In Douglas's opinion, experience will bring sophistication to a multiple killer's methods, and this is certainly a description that can be applied to Chapman. He was clearly an intelligent man and was on a learning curve.

On balance then, was this man Jack the Ripper? Unlike most other suggested subjects, he is a known killer, living in the right place at the right time. So, yes ladies and gentlemen, I offer you Severin Klosowski, aka George Chapman, as Jack the Ripper.

Epilogue

So what became of Lucy Baderski and her daughter Cecilia Klosowski?

Around 1898, Lucy met a fellow Pole, a cabinet maker, and together they had a son in 1899. They were living in Limehouse. They married in June 1903, two months after Chapman was hung, and went on to have four more children. By 1911 the family had moved to Poplar.[44]

Cecilia married in 1908. She was seventeen; her husband being fourteen years her senior. Their marriage certificate shows that she was living in Poplar at the time of her union and that her husband came from Whitechapel. They had five children together, moving after the birth of the second child from Whitechapel to West Ham.[45]

Endnotes

1. Adam, H. L., *Trial of George Chapman (Notable British Trials Series)* (William Hodge & Co., 1930), pp.219–223
2. *ibid.*, p.63
3. *ibid.*, p.64
4. Marriage certificate
5. Birth & Death certificates
6. *Trial of George Chapman (Notable British Trials Series)*, p.65
7. Birth certificate
8. *Trial of George Chapman (Notable British Trials Series)*, p.65
9. Birth certificate
10. *Trial of George Chapman (Notable British Trials Series)*, p.101
11. *ibid.*, p.203
12. *ibid.*, p.123
13. *ibid.*, p.203
14. *ibid.*, p.205
15. *ibid.*, p.207
16. *ibid.*, p.211
17. *ibid.*, pp.133–34
18. *ibid.*, pp.140–43
19. *ibid.*, p.72
20. *ibid.*, pp.98–100
21. *ibid.*, p.170
22. *ibid.*, p.189
23. *ibid.*, p.104
24. *ibid.*, p.73
25. *ibid.*, p.82

26. *ibid.*, pp.102–3
27. *ibid.*, p.91
28. *ibid.*, p.107
29. *ibid.*, p.146
30. *ibid.*, p.148
31. *ibid.*, p.198
32. *ibid.*, p.57
33. *ibid.*, pp.68-71
34. *ibid.*, p.59
35. *ibid.*, p.33–4
36. *ibid.*, pp.91–6
37. *ibid.*, pp.152–64
38. *ibid.*, p.164
39. *ibid.*, p.63
40. Birth certificate
41. *Trial of George Chapman (Notable British Trials Series)*, p.65
42. Birth certificate
43. *Trial of George Chapman (Notable British Trials Series)*, p.65
44. Birth certificate; Marriage certificate; Census
45. *ibid.*

Bibliography

Adam, H. L., *Trial of George Chapman (Notable British Trials Series)*, (William Hodge & Co., 1930)

Susan Parry is a retired deputy head teacher of a secondary school and is now teaching mathematics part-time. She has been a member of The Whitechapel Society since the very beginning and took on the role of secretary, and later treasurer, in 2006. Sue lives in Norfolk with her husband Phil, a chartered accountant, and they have three children and four grandchildren.

4

More likely than Cutbush: Montague John Druitt

Adrian Morris

In February 1894, an article appeared in a British newspaper claiming to be an exposé on the real identity of a murderer who had been known to the world as Jack the Ripper. These articles, produced in The *Sun* newspaper, would be serialised for a number of issues.

They generated great interest and aroused the suspicions of the police, who realised that the arrest of this suspect, in 1891, could have had more to it, which might, in turn, make it worthwhile following up on The *Sun*'s investigation. The suspect in question was Thomas Hayne Cutbush. He had been arrested for assaulting a female victim and attempting to assault another by violent attacks with a knife, which he had purchased in Houndsditch. The case resulted in his apprehension and permanent detention in Broadmoor, in 1891.

There was serious concern that the then Home Secretary, the future Prime Minister H.H. Asquith, would be bombarded with questions in Parliament as a result of The *Sun*'s articles. In 1894, it eventually fell to the Chief Constable of the Metropolitan Police, Melville Macnaghten, to compile a memorandum to provide the Home Secretary with more essential information about both the Cutbush and the Jack the Ripper cases.

Melville Macnaghten appeared to consult a number of documents – albeit casually in some cases – and, possibly, used remembered details from previous readings or briefings before referring to the original case notes on the Cutbush case in compiling his memoranda in 1894. It must be stressed that this document was private, and the information was only meant to be used, if the Home Secretary needed to fall back on it to satisfy Parliament of The *Sun's* allegations being unfounded.

An interesting, and indeed vital, aspect of Macnaghten's Memoranda

Montague John Druitt. Previously unpublished photograph. (By permission of Winchester College Archives)

was that he looked at a number of suspects who had been in the minds of the higher echelons of the Metropolitan Police during, or after, the Whitechapel Murders investigation. Macnaghten's aim was to prove, to the Home Secretary, that there were better Jack the Ripper suspects than Thomas Cutbush.

'I may mention the cases of three men, any one of whom would have been more likely than Cutbush to have committed this series of murders...' So began a pivotal sentence in one of the draft documents that made up part of Macnaghten's Memoranda. Macnaghten would go on to name his three most likely suspects who were better placed, in his mind at least, to be the Whitechapel murderer. His second and third suspects were men who were, at one time, on the police files, as there had been some serious investigations carried out upon them.

One of the suspects, Michael Ostrog, was a highly disreputable character. He was originally from the Russian Empire and was known to assume a wide variety of aliases in the commission of his, often, outlandish crimes. The other suspect was a local man called Kosminski, who had been detained in a lunatic asylum some years after the murders, but had fallen under some suspicion from the police in the immediate period following the murders. The main suspect on Macnaghten's list – a suspect that he would favour as being the best candidate for being Jack the Ripper – was a man called Montague John Druitt.

Macnaghten, in one of the two existing versions of the memoranda (there was some evidence that a third version existed), said of Druitt:

> Mr M.J. Druitt a doctor of about forty-one years of age and of fairly good family, who disappeared at the time of the Miller's Court Murder, and whose body was found floating in the Thames on 31st Dec: i.e. 7 weeks after the said murder. The body was said to have been in the water for a month, or more – on it was found a season ticket between Blackheath & London. From private information I have little doubt but that his own family suspected this man of being the Whitechapel murderer; it was alleged that he was sexually insane.

Interesting reading; Macnaghten obviously saw the suspicion against Druitt as pretty powerful, to the point of making Druitt his prime suspect.

What do we make of Macnaghten's suspicion of Montague John Druitt? It is interesting that Macnaghten refers to 'private information' which threw this suspect's name within the sweep of his suspicion. Macnaghten also talks of the family's suspicion against Druitt, claiming they thought he was Jack the Ripper. This would suggest that Macnaghten may have received this information from the family of Druitt. Certainly – and this is a continuing matter of conjecture – Macnaghten's view that Druitt was a primary suspect is at odds with the opinions of the rest of the police hierarchy who were, in many cases, better placed than he was to assign suspicion on this suspect or that. Some did this, as with the official head of the investigation, Dr Robert Anderson, who was the Assistant Commissioner of the Metropolitan Police force in 1888. He went for Kosminski, another suspect mentioned in Macnaghten's Memoranda. Other police officials engaged in the case, such as Inspector Abberline, would refute any suspicion against Druitt. Druitt seems to have been introduced by Macnaghten alone, as there really was no consensus among the police, in 1888, as to who the Whitechapel murderer might have been.

The 'private information' Macnaghten refers to and the fact that 'his [Druitt's] own family suspected' that he could have been Jack the Ripper, implies that Druitt's family made this information known to Macnaghten themselves, or through a third party. Remember, the details of the Macnaghten's Memoranda were strictly private and never meant for public consumption. There is some evidence to show that the Druitt family had links to a set of families known as the Elton and Mayo families, respectively. They would maintain strong links, even after many of them had emigrated to Australia in the nineteenth century. It is interesting to note that the private secretary to the then Commissioner of the Metropolitan Police, Sir Charles Warren, in 1888 – during the Whitechapel Murders – was Walter Ernest Boultbee. Boultbee was married to Ellen Baker, a niece of Alfred Mayo, who was himself related to Montague John Druitt's father, Thomas. Also, Macnaghten's father seems to have had some dealings with the Druitt family at some official (and possibly private) level. This could possibly explain Macnaghten's 'private information', and how he came by it.

When looking closely at what Macnaghten says about his prime suspect Druitt, we can see he gets a number of key things incorrect. Macnaghten's Memoranda is strewn with unintentional errors; they are minor in most instances, but it makes one feel that he was compiling the information largely from memory or remembrances of briefings and documents he may have consulted a good deal of time before. It is of interest to note that when writing his memoirs *Days of My Years*, in 1913, Macnaghten ruefully yielded to the reliance on memory and recollections rather than consult detailed notes. Errors pertaining to Druitt's age and profession are among the most obvious. Druitt was thirty-one years old, not forty-one. He was a barrister and school master not a doctor. One would expect – it would not be too difficult to concede – that if Macnaghten had been consulting a document detailing certain suspicions on Druitt contained in the police or Home Office files, he might have recorded these fundamentals accurately. Reaching into the penumbra of his mind, Macnaghten may even have got Druitt's first name wrong on another variant version of this memorandum, referring to him as Michael. This does not necessarily preclude the existence of a police file on Druitt, but the specific language used by Macnaghten to describe the suspects Kosminski and Ostrog was more typical of a police report. We know that both these suspects were under some kind of police suspicion during the wider Whitechapel Murders investigation. Intriguingly, Macnaghten has a more accurate grasp on the details surrounding Druitt's suicide, referring to possessions found on Druitt's body: 'season ticket between Blackheath & London.'

Interestingly, Macnaghten refers to Druitt as having been 'sexually insane'. This is a rather peculiar pronouncement because it would appear to account, at first glance, for Druitt's suspicion of being the Whitechapel murderer. However, often the term 'sexually insane', when used in its late Victorian context, intimated that someone was believed to be a 'sexual deviant' or homosexual. This was the period following the passing of the 1885 Criminal Law Amendment Act, which enshrined the illegality of sexual acts between males, making it a criminal act punishable with a custodial sentence.

Another indictment of Druitt's alleged mental state, following his death, was the Coroner's jury finding his death to be a result of 'suicide whilst of unsound mind'. Suicide, although more sympathetically viewed by the late Victorians, was still outlawed and maintained some of the old stigma it had in previous generations. Overwhelmingly, suicide could be seen as an act of madness at one end of the scale, or desperation at the other, but was still labelled 'unsound mind'.

The Coroner's inquest also dug deeper into Druitt's circumstances prior to his death. He had been a schoolmaster at Mr George Valentine's school, in Blackheath, from 1880. It transpired that he had been dismissed by Valentine on 30 November, shortly before his suicide, for getting into 'serious trouble' at the school. Again, the full nature of this serious trouble has been open to conjecture; however, many feel it could possibly have involved unsuitable conduct against one of the pupils there. The school itself was an all-male establishment, which was a sort of finishing school for older boys preparing for university and the army – basically, the Victorian elite. This is an obvious conclusion to make, but there is nothing to back it up. Merely coupling it with Macnaghten's term, 'sexual insanity' does not necessarily apply to his dismissal, but it may be more relevant to Druitt's perceived guilt of being a sexual serial murderer of women.

So, it is to Macnaghten's accusation of guilt towards Druitt that we must look. The 'private information' is mentioned in the same sentence as the family's belief that Druitt was the Ripper. We can only wonder at what this might be and accept speculations, as I have done previously. A powerful reason for suspecting Druitt was the timing of his suicide, in late November/early December 1888; perfect for the traditionally accepted – but not universally so – final murder in the Ripper series; that of Mary Kelly in early November. Macnaghten would highlight this point in another part of his memoranda, when he theorised that '...the ripper (sic) brain gave way altogether after his glut in Miller's Court and that he then committed suicide.' Elsewhere Macnaghten would go on to add, '...the more I think the matter over, the stronger do these opinions become.'

The mere circumstance and timing of his death has, undoubtedly, made Montague John Druitt one of the most persistent of all suspects since he was fully revealed to the wider world in the 1950s. This has been given extra buoyancy by the forceful fact that a high-ranking police official, although one who did not take part in the Whitechapel murder investigation in 1888, named Druitt as a subject in a clandestine report.

Nevertheless, Druitt's suicide, although exquisitely timed for the assumed ending of the murder series in late 1888, is still the only real circumstantial evidence we have against Druitt. The thoroughly impenetrable 'private information' from Druitt's family, which might yield more detailed investigation and debate, is mere speculation. Of course, added to these complexities, we must always acknowledge the *sine qua non* that all Jack the Ripper suspects must display a seriously valid account for the abrupt ending of the murder series. Druitt fits into this very well.

It is only fair then, to look deeper into the real element of the pertinacity of suspicion against Druitt – his suicide. Aside from the difficulty in establishing a proper and detailed examination of the familial insights, we must assume that the major suspicion against Druitt is predicated on his suicide. Taking out of the equation the sophistry of murder upon Druitt, it is his suicide that we must account for.

If Druitt was Jack the Ripper, his suicide is easily explained. As Macnaghten said, by associational intimation, Druitt's mind seemed to have given way 'after his awful glut in Miller's Court...' Therefore, remorse took hold of him and he took the only way out, as he saw it. Some serial killers may attempt suicide, but there are many more that do not.

A more viable explanation for Druitt's suicide may be more obvious; namely, the circumstances surrounding his dismissal from Mr Valentine's school. One might assume – and assumption it is – that if Druitt had been involved in an illegal act of a sexual nature, he may have lost the rigid *esprit de corps* amongst his peers. Druitt did, however, seemingly avoid arrest for this 'serious trouble' and was only dismissed. Of course, we can only assume that this was the reason for his dismissal – there is no shred of evidence to confirm it. Other viable reasons could equally be a conflict with Mr Valentine, or theft, or dereliction of duty. This still brings us back to the subject of Druitt's suicide, and ultimately how it fits into any significant suspicion against him.

Depression can be a major cause of suicide, especially amongst young men. Druitt seems more likely to have been going through some personal turmoil; as such a suicide would indicate. It is a reasonable scenario that dismissal from the school could have been related to depression; it could have been affecting Druitt's mental equilibrium and conduct at the school, or the cordiality of his relations with his employer, Mr Valentine. Being in the employ of such an establishment as Mr Valentine's, despite its low pay and Druitt's other activities, shows a man who had actively tried to engage himself within a rigid social circle of people. Such a fracturing of these relations, as a result of depression or such related problems, could have caused ostracisation for Druitt; as the Victorian elite looked to avoid association with the 'mentally' ill. This, in turn, could only have compounded Druitt's problems.

There is additional evidence that Druitt was suffering from serious depression; amongst his possessions in his room was a suicide note, in the form of a letter addressed to his elder brother, William. In this letter he indicated the reason for his decision to take his own life: 'Since Friday I felt that I was going to be like mother, and it would be best for all concerned if I were to die.' Far from explicating reasons for being a serial killer, the note actually points very strongly to personal reasons for his suicide and being in a depressed state of mind.

Druitt's mother had been confined to an asylum in July 1888, following a serious bout of depression, which seemed to be aggravated by her husband's death in 1885. It had been a suicide attempt, in 1888, which initiated the decision to place her in an asylum in Clapton, where she was certified insane. Her mental state had been exacerbated by her suffering from the, then untreatable, condition diabetes. This was, seemingly, hereditary in the Druitt family. It is an interesting point that whilst Druitt's mother and an aunt attempted suicide, his maternal grandmother and his eldest sister both actually committed suicide. These were less enlightened times, as mentioned before, when the notion of suicide was seen as both a sign of weakness in person and, more specifically, mind. There were no support agencies to help cope with such desires, and no benevolent approaches from groups within authority to address such an issue. Druitt's depressed mental state, in late 1888, could undoubtedly have been influenced by the prospect that he might end up as his mother had – either attempting suicide or being committed to a mental institution. Druitt's case, in 1888, seems to highlight the extreme prejudice with which Victorian society viewed not only suicides, but also cases of mental infirmity, which today would be deemed as treatable. Such prejudices, then, could begin to explain the formulation of a familial suspicion against Druitt, although, how this gets linked with his potential for being the Whitechapel murderer is still far from clear.

An interesting aspect of Druitt's professional life, in 1888, and one that might explain a lot of the events that surrounded his potential decision to commit suicide, is his second career. It has often been described by scholars on this subject that Druitt was a failed barrister. This, simply, is not the case. He actively maintained chambers at a practise address at No.9 King's Bench Walk, in the illustrious Temple area of London, which was at the heart of the legal profession. Druitt had been active in highly demanding cases in the late 1880s, and seemed to show a tremendous degree of skill in successfully completing them. We must remember that he came from a semi-legal family and his older brother had a successful legal practice in Bournemouth.

One case that Druitt fought, in September 1888, during the Whitechapel murder scare, was at the Old Bailey itself. The case was one concerned with the malicious wounding of Peter Black by a former friend, Christopher Power, in the Kilburn area of London, in August 1888. Druitt, acting as defence counsel, realised the untenable nature of a 'not guilty' verdict based on the simple aspects of the case. Druitt instead pushed for a plea of insanity. He was also up against the formidable Charles Frederick Gill, acting for the prosecution as Senior Counsel for the Post Office, as there was evidence of some use of obscene letters by the accused.

With a great degree of skill and persuasive arguing, Druitt essentially 'won' the case with a successful 'guilty, but insane' verdict. Not only does this case, amongst the many others he fought during this period, show that Druitt was becoming a proficient and expert legal practitioner, he was also conducting this particularly stressful case during a period in which many have argued he could have been Jack the Ripper.

Montague John Druitt. (Moody/ Morris Collection)

Druitt committed suicide in early December 1888. This is an obvious fact that we know about this rather enigmatic person, while there is a distinct dearth of knowledge about his private life, which mere speculation can only assume. However, there are rather telling features in the court case concerning, Christopher Power, in September 1888. The details of the case illustrated that the defendant Christopher Power was suffering some form of mental illness. This was affecting his work as a draughtsman and he was dismissed from his employment for 'slackness' and conflict with fellow workers in the same establishment. One of his colleagues, Peter Black – a former friend – Power later decided to attack both verbally, via obscene letters and innuendo, and ultimately violently by use of a knife. Obviously, without reference to elements of the Ripper case, let us restrict ourselves to Druitt's personal world. The situation Power found himself in September 1888, in the mental aspect at least, was not unlike the situation Druitt would find himself in a few months later; which culminated in his suicide.

Power was eventually committed to an asylum, due to his 'guilty, but insane' plea that Druitt had worked for. Is it not possible that Druitt's world was seemingly beginning to mirror Power's in certain aspects, albeit without the obvious violent overtones? Certainly, as we saw earlier, Druitt did, as a matter of documented fact, believe his mental state was weakening for he left a note proclaiming so: 'Since Friday I felt I was going to be like mother...'

We can speculate on the specific events that took place on that previous Friday, but it is more than possible it may have involved a visit to his mother, or some such related episode on behalf of his mother who was residing in an asylum in Clapton.

I would therefore say that Druitt was probably suffering from depression; a common reason for suicide. Of course, without the benefit of medical examinations and opinion (Druitt seems not to have been under any such observation) we can not be specific on his actual mental health in late 1888, but I do advance that he was suffering from depression, possibly aggravated by the sometimes extreme pressure on him from all areas of his life, not least a demanding and stressful career in the legal profession.

In the late nineteenth century the study of mental illness, despite the introduction of maiden treatments and continued academic discourse, was still in its infancy. We may wonder that in our 'advanced' age, the mysteries of the mind might still set us at the foothills of knowledge. For a man like Druitt, in 1888, engaged in a world of reputations and social climbing, maintaining a strict social contract, meant that he had to keep up appearances and take on responsibilities within a rigid class system, even at the acceptance of a relatively low-paid job at Mr Valentine's educational institution. For men like Druitt status was all. Nevertheless, he would have felt that he had to traverse such a system to reach a position that gave him the social standing he needed and desired. As we have seen, a burgeoning legal career was growing into a very successful one by the end of 1888, allowing him to earn much more money than in his official job with Valentine. This may have caused friction with Mr Valentine, leading to an argument and ultimately his dismissal, made worse by his weakened mental state.

If we take into account the lack of support for those suffering from depression in Victorian London, coupled with the self-doubt a young man like Druitt would have had, we see the significance of his dismissal. It meant he was cut off from all he wanted to be. Before he was a peer and even influential amongst the Victorian elite and so his enforced ostracisation was the death knell to this depressed, young social climber. At the same time, Druitt could not have accepted such a course of action on his own; it was for others to initiate like his family and friends. In Druitt's personal circumstances in 1888, although surrounded by copious work colleagues in his day-to-day activities, his eventual dismissal from Valentine's school isolated him. This seems to be a more likely reason for Druitt's suicide in late 1888. However, some still feel he could be Jack the Ripper because, as a suspect, he 'was more likely than Cutbush!'

Bibliography

Begg, P., Fido, M. & Skinner, K., *The Jack the Ripper A–Z* (Headline, 1996)

Adrian Morris hails from Neasden in north-west London. He was born only a stone's throw from Dollis Hill House, where both the great Victorian Prime Minister William Gladstone and the brilliant American writer Mark Twain once lived. He studied Political Science at Birkbeck College, London University, and has a long-standing interest in Irish history and post-1945 American history. He is a founding member of The Whitechapel Society and has been the editor of its journal since its modern inception in 2005.

5

Sir William Gull

M.J. Trow

'Since every Jack became a gentleman, there's many a gentle person made a Jack.'
(Shakespeare, *Richard III*, Act I, Sc. 3)

The Facts

William Withey Gull was born aboard the *Dove*, a barge owned by his father, John, on the last day of 1816, while they were moored at St Osyth Mill, Colchester. John Gull was a wharfinger – a man who made his living ferrying cargo between Colchester and the Thames; William was the youngest of eight children. When he was four, the family moved to Thorpe-le-Soken in Essex. Within five years, John had died from cholera; a new epidemic sweeping London in those years.

It was William's mother, Elizabeth, a devout and hardworking woman, who was responsible for her children's education. She inspired her youngest to become a pupil teacher (one of the few ways upward for a working-class child), studying Latin and Greek. Through a local connection – Benjamin Harrison was a neighbour of the Gulls and Treasurer of Guys Hospital – the twenty-one-year-old joined the hospital as a medical student, with two rooms and a yearly income of £50.

He was very bright and exceptionally hard working, obtaining his first degree (by convention a BA), in 1838. He obtained his MB (Bachelor of Medicine) three years later and was lecturing in *Materia Medica* (Pharmacology) at Guys a year after that. He became MD, in 1846, and for the next three years was Fullerian Professor of Physiology, during which time he became friends with the scientist Michael Faraday.

In 1848, while Europe convulsed with revolution and the Chartists met on Kennington Common in London, William Gull married Susan Lacy, the daughter of an army colonel from Carlisle. The young couple moved to genteel premises in Finsbury Square and Susan gave birth to three children over the next twelve years. Caroline was born in 1851 and William nine years later. The third child, Cameron, probably born in 1858, died in infancy.

By the year of his marriage, Gull had become a Fellow of the Royal College of Physicians and, by 1869, was a Fellow of the Royal Society. He lectured regularly and was at the cutting edge of research, turning him into an international star in medical circles. He was an expert in myxoedema (thyroid problems), Bright's disease (a disease of the kidneys), paraplegia and anorexia (it was Gull who first coined the term).

What really made Gull's name, however, was his treatment of the Prince of Wales, when he suffered from the life-threatening typhus fever in 1871. 'Bertie's' father, Albert, had died of the disease ten years earlier and Victoria was distraught, in case another member of her family should go the same way. Bertie recovered – *The Times* describing his care as 'nursing so tender, ministry so minute'– and the grateful Queen made Gull one of her four Physicians-in-

Ordinary and a baronet. He was now First Baronet Gull of Brook Street, a far more imposing address than Finsbury Square and his coat-of-arms is a true Victorian monstrosity, in-keeping with the poor heraldic artwork of the time.

Throughout the 1870s and 1880s, honours continued to be heaped on Gull. He received honorary degrees from Oxford, Cambridge and Edinburgh universities and sat on the General Medical Council. He championed the cause of women in medicine (there were no female doctors in his day) and worked with his usual passion and enthusiasm until 1887, when he suffered a stroke at his Scottish retreat, Urrard House, in Killiecrankie. The cerebral haemorrhage had caused, in medical terms, hemiplegia (paralysis of one side of the body – in Gull's case, his right) and aphasia (loss of speech). He recovered sufficiently to work in his London practice but knew it was the beginning of the end. 'One arrow had missed its mark,' he wrote, 'but there are more in the quiver.'

He was right. After a third stroke, he died at 12.30 p.m. on 30 January 1890. He was seventy-four. Gull was buried in the family plot, in the parish churchyard at Thorpe-le-Soken, next to his parents. A special train had to be laid on to bring all the mourners from London. Eulogies came from all over the world – the American novelist Mark Twain noted the death in his diary – and on the headstone they carved the lines:

> What doth the Lord require of thee but to do justly and to love mercy and to walk humbly with God?

All in all, a well respected gentleman. William Gull's story can hardly be called conventional. From humble beginnings, he made his mark in medical science and can stand alongside the great doctors – not just of his day but of all time.

Then, eighty years after his death, someone claimed that he was Jack the Ripper.

The Fantasy

William Gull belongs to that strand of Ripperology involving the highest in the land. The logic (if it can be called that) runs something like this: a maniac killed a disputed number of women in the East End of London, in 1888, and was never caught. Why not? Because there was a huge cover-up. Who could have orchestrated such a cover-up? It had to be someone in the corridors of power, with supreme clout. Who could that be? Someone closely connected with the Royal Family – the highest in the land.

The proverbial Elephant in the room, in respect of the Whitechapel Murders, is the likelihood that the killer had some medical expertise; evident, not in the killings, but in the post-mortem mutilations and removal of organs. Various police surgeons at the time – Thomas Bond and Frederick Brown were the most impressive – could not believe that a surgeon, having taken the Hippocratic Oath to save life, could carry out such crimes at all. Clearly, they had no notion of the impulses that drive a serial killer and were unaware of the depressingly long list of murderous doctors from William Palmer to Harold Shipman. They were probably right about the mutilations however; a practising surgeon had ample opportunity to cut and remove organs on a daily basis, without resorting to the dingy alleyways of the Abyss.

But of course, in the case of the highest in the land, we are not talking about cold, rational fact, based on historical and empirical research, but a myriad of conspiracy theories.

In the world of the mythological Ripper, William Gull fits like a hand in a glove. However much we try to shake it off, the image of the top-hat, cape and medical-bag-carrying monster will not disappear into the (equally irrelevant) London fog. As a Fellow of the Royal College of Physicians and the Queen's doctor, of course, he wore those clothes and he would have carried a medical bag.

Gull's name first appears linked with the Ripper in *The Criminologist*, in November 1970, in an article written by Dr Thomas Stowell. To be fair to Stowell, his article was called 'Jack the Ripper – a Solution?', with the all-important question mark, and it was other Ripperologists who sought to put flesh on the bones and replace healthy scepticism with dogmatic certainty. Stowell had been a friend and medical partner of Dr Theodore Dyke Acland, Gull's son-in-law. He believed that the Ripper was 'Eddie' (Prince Albert Victor, the Duke of Clarence), Victoria's grandson and heir to the throne. There is little doubt that Stowell was more than a little confused. He claimed that Gull had been seen in the Whitechapel area on more than one occasion, and was there shadowing the deranged Eddie, in order to certify him insane prior to his being locked away in an institution. Stowell was eighty-five when he wrote the article, which was heavily amended by the editor, and he died in the same year. Certainly his conversations with criminologist Colin Wilson show a scant regard for the facts. When his article, suggesting a royal connection, appeared, Stowell wrote a retraction to *The Times*, claiming that he was both a Royalist and a loyalist. But the damage had been done; Ripperology, with all its delicious and infuriating red herrings, took off from this point.

William Gull moved from accessory after the fact, to protagonist three years later. Joseph Gorman Sickert, who claimed to be the son of the Victorian painter Walter Sickert, contributed to a BBC drama documentary and his story was seized upon by journalist, Stephen Knight in what is still, probably, the best known book on the case – *Jack the Ripper: The Final Solution*.

In a long (and unbelievable) story cut short, Knight asserted that Eddie had married a Catholic shopgirl (Annie Elizabeth Crook) and her friends, led by Mary Kelly, tried to blackmail the government to keep the scandal secret. A worried Prime Minister (Lord Salisbury), anxious to save the Royal Family's face, and to prevent a potential collapse of government, called in his old Freemason friend, William Gull, to silence Kelly and co. in any way he saw fit. Because Gull had medical training, he could kill easily with a surgeon's knife and he left Masonic ritual mutilations as a warning to others. To explain how an eminent physician could track down the women concerned, find his way around Whitechapel and get

Sir William Gull.
(Copyright Control)

The Spiritualist medium, Robert James Lees.

away unobserved, Sickert and Knight brought in a coachman, John Netley. Netley not only drove the doctor to the murder sites, but allowed the killings to take place in his cab. With Walter Sickert – who knew Mary Kelly personally – as lookout (Joseph Sickert claimed that this was actually Robert Anderson, head of the CID), the Ripper became not one man, but three. All with the aim to conceal the terrible secret of the clandestine marriage, and the birth of a daughter (Alice Crook) who, it could be argued, should have become Queen of England.

Further 'evidence' against Gull comes from a rather tortuous source. Articles began to appear in various American newspapers, including the *Chicago Sunday Times Herald* in April 1895, claiming that the Ripper was an eminent London doctor. The information came from tittle-tattle from Dr Benjamin Howard, an American who had been working in London, and he had told the story to a prominent San Francisco citizen, William Greer Harrison. Although the doctor was unnamed, there were sufficient links with Guys Hospital – and the vivisectionist lobby, of which Gull was a member – for the well-informed to draw obvious conclusions. Even though Howard wrote a strenuous denial, via the *People* in January1896, to the effect that he had never discussed Jack the Ripper with anyone and knew no more than the sketchy newspaper reports back in 1888, the public were hooked.

The same series of articles concerned the spiritualist medium Robert James Lees, who claimed to have offered his services to both the City and Metropolitan Police in early October, 1888. Lees' story was that whilst riding on a bus, he had the strongest sensation that he was sitting near the Ripper. He followed his suspect to an elegant house in the West End (later said to be Brook Street), and this led to police questioning the inhabitants. Lees' fellow traveller turned out to be William Gull, who had recently suffered from serious bouts of memory loss. Over a period of time, the physician's wife had come to recognise her husband's increasingly violent mood swings and had become so afraid of him that she had locked herself, and her children, in a room in the house. At one point, she discovered blood on her husband's shirt for which he could not account. A court of inquiry was held by Gull's fellow doctors (or Masons, or both, depending on which subsequent version of the tale you read) and, convinced of his guilt, they sentenced him to an asylum under the pseudonym 'Thomas Mason 124'. The word was put out that Gull had died, but the coffin contained either another body entirely or a pile of rocks, depending on how far down the conspiratorial path you want to go.

Nothing is more delicious to a researcher, especially of conspiracy theories, than to stumble upon a collection of papers which blow the lid off an accepted body of evidence. When Frank Spiering wrote *Prince Jack* in 1978, some of the material for the book came from the Academy of Medicine Library, in New York. This was a straight, 1896, reprint of the memoirs that had appeared two years earlier, written by Dr Acland, Gull's son-in-law. What intrigued Spiering was the sheaf of 120 handwritten pages – apparently in Gull's handwriting – which contained the extraordinary information that Gull had told the Prince of Wales that his son, Eddie, was dying from tertiary syphilis. Even more bizarre was the claim that Gull had hypnotised Eddie, and the heir to the throne had confessed to the Whitechapel Murders. He had become aroused watching butchers at work in Aldgate High Street, and had taken a knife to commit the crimes from the horse slaughterers in Buck's Row (technically, the firm of Harrison in Winthrop Street). The Prince complained of headaches and was very talkative, showing signs of slight delirium. He also had a leather apron in his possession, a positive link to the notion of the butcher and one of the most famous red herrings in the entire Ripper case. In this version of the tale, of course, the Ripper is not Gull, but Eddie, and once again the Queen's physician assumes the role of accessory after the fact.

Scratching around for circumstantial evidence, various commentators have hit upon 'the grape theory', which has resurfaced in more than one movie about Jack. In one of these, Gull uses poisoned grapes to lull his victims into a stupor before killing and mutilating them in his coach. According to Stephen Knight, Gull was a great believer in grapes as refreshment when tired, but the idea that he constantly carried a bunch with him seems a little unlikely. Poison of course is pre-eminently the doctor's murder weapon, in fact as well as fiction, so this makes sense. In fact, it makes no sense at all. The publicity-seeking grocer, Matthew Packer, whose shop was close to Dutfield's Yard in Berner Street, claimed to have sold a bunch of grapes to a man accompanying Liz Stride, shortly before she was murdered. Witnesses at the scene later – Louis Diemschutz, Isaac Kozebrodski, Fanny Mortimer and Eva Harstein – all claimed to have seen a grape stem in or near the dead woman's hand. The police and doctors, who were called to Dutfield's Yard (men trained to be observant), saw nothing of the kind, only the cachous (sweets) in Liz Stride's left hand. At the inquest, Drs Bagster-Phillips and Blackwell swore that there were no grapes at the crime scene and none in the stomach of the deceased. Even if both these doctors were wrong, of course, it does not remotely point a finger at Gull, or anyone else in the medical profession. We might as well point the finger at the story-changing Matthew Packer.

Clutching at straws, other Ripperologists have pointed out that William Gull was a supporter of vivisection – the carrying out of experiments on animals for scientific purposes. This has been alleged as an example of his cruelty, but takes things entirely out of context. England has always had an animal-centric culture (the Royal Society for the Prevention of Cruelty to Animals was established forty years before the National Society for the Prevention of Cruelty to Children, for example), but conversely, bad treatment of animals, especially horses, was commonplace and in all his writings, Gull put people first rather than animals second. Even if he was particularly callous in this regard (and there was no evidence for this), the leap of logic that he must be the Whitechapel murderer is extraordinary.

Then we have the fact that Gull delivered the Goulstonian Lectures at Guys Hospital, with all the delicious associations with Goulston Street and the irrelevant 'Juwes' graffito. Dr Goulston was actually a seventeenth-century physician and that, rather than the street, is the only link.

The case against Gull rests entirely on the royal connection, and I do not have the space in this chapter to demolish that nonsense; except to say that all the theories emanating from Sickert and Knight have been discredited by painstaking research. Psychological profilers, over the last thirty years, have established the likelihood that the Ripper was an asocial loner whose sexual activity may have involved prostitutes. He probably came from the same social class as his victims and would have passed unnoticed in the streets of Whitechapel, which he clearly knew very well. Geo-profilers would add that Jack killed in his 'circle of comfort', which again points us to the Abyss. None of this fits William Gull, at all. He was a doctor, but not a surgeon. He worked in Guys Hospital, which is half an hour's walk from Whitechapel and south of the river, well out of any geo-profiler circle of comfort. There is nothing to connect Gull with the Abyss, except the highly tenuous links via Walter Sickert and his supposed studio in Cleveland Street (which did not exist either!), as told to Ripperologist Jean Overton Fuller, by Sickert's friend Florence Pash.

The whole tale of the mad Mason, whisking Annie Crook off to a private asylum and operating on her to remove her memory, is high melodrama but has absolutely no basis in fact. Neither was Gull an expert on syphilis, and if he did recommend the use of mercury as a potential cure for the disease, he went along with 90 per cent of the medical profession at the time. How the twenty-four-year-old Eddie was supposed to be suffering from tertiary syphilis, when that stage usually takes fifteen years to develop, has never been explained. Gull was never a Freemason, so the 'highest in the land theory' collapses on that score alone, making a similar nonsense of the pseudonym Thomas Mason – the name given for Gull's supposed incarceration in an asylum, following the Ripper Murders.

The only 'evidence' against Gull – and it is flimsy in the extreme – rests on the claims of Robert Lees and the supposed police visit to Gull's house, in Brook Street. Everything else – the memory lapses, the mood swings, the bloody shirt, the unofficial doctors' 'jury' and the fake funeral – is just smoke and mirrors. There is no mention, in any police record, of Lees offering his services to them, nor were there any enquiries in Brook Street or the involvement of a doctor named Gull. The so-called corroborative evidence, provided by Stephen Knight, of a letter sent by a crank in July 1889, is a simple misreading: 'With all your "Lees", with all your blue bottles...', should actually read 'tecs' (i.e. detectives). Without that all-important police corroboration, all we have is the speculative nonsense that has been launched against an innocent man for forty years.

Those who put Gull in the frame, from Dr Stowell to today's filmmakers, should have read the words of the great doctor, recorded for posterity in 1894: 'Fools and savages explain; wise men investigate.'

Mei Trow is a member of the Society of Authors, Crime Writers' Association and Welsh Academy. He has over fifty books to his credit, both fiction and non-fiction, and has written extensively on Jack the Ripper. He has lectured to The Whitechapel Society and has appeared in a number of Jack-related documentaries.

6

The Mysteries of Aaron Kosminski

Philip Marquis

The elderly man had been absorbed in the book from the very beginning, but when he reached page 137, his pulse began to quicken as he read the words, 'and the conclusion we came to was that he and his people were certain low class polish Jews...'

He nodded in agreement and turned the page. Excitement surged within him as he read on. When he came to the passage, 'I will merely add that the only person who ever had a good view of the murderer unhesitatingly identified the suspect the instant he was confronted with him, but he refused to give evidence against him', he could contain himself no longer and, picking up a pencil, he scrawled underneath:

> ...because the suspect was also a Jew and also because his evidence would convict the suspect and witness would be the means of murderer being hanged which he did not wish to be left on his mind. DSS

Splaying out into the left-hand margin of the page, 'DSS' continued, 'and after this identification which suspect knew, no other murder of this kind took place in London.'

Running out of space now, he turned to the end of the book, changed pencils, and wrote on one of the endpapers:

> After the suspect had been identified, by us, at the seaside home where he had been sent by us with difficulty, in order to subject him to identification and he knew he was identified.
>
> On suspect's return to his brother's house in White-chapel he was watched by police [City CID] by day and night. In a very short time the suspect with his hands tied behind his back he was sent to Stepney Workhouse and then to Colney Hatch and died shortly afterwards – Kosminski was the suspect – DSS

'DSS' stood for Donald Sutherland Swanson, a retired Detective Chief Inspector of the Metropolitan Police who, in 1888, had been in charge of the day-to-day running of the Ripper investigation. The book in which he was making notes, *The Lighter Side of My Official Life*, by Swanson's old boss, Assistant Commissioner (CID) Sir Robert Anderson, was published in 1910, when Swanson was sixty-two and Anderson, sixty-nine. The man Swanson had named was Aaron Mordke Kosminski, a Polish Jew from the province of Kalish. At the time Swanson was annotating the book, he believed Kosminski was dead. However, he was in fact alive and resident in the Leavesden home for imbeciles, although his incarceration there might fairly be described as a living death.

But, it is Anderson's number two in the 1890s, Chief Constable Sir Melville Macnaghten, who we have to thank for first bringing Kosminski's name to our attention. In 1894, he was

Popular depiction of Aaron Kosminski.
(*Illustrated London News*, 1888)

asked to prepare a report for the Home Office on Thomas Cutbush, a man named as the Ripper in a series of newspaper articles. In his report, Macnaghten exonerated Cutbush and mentioned three men whom he thought were more likely to have been the killer. One of these three was Aaron Kosminski.

There are two extant versions of the Macnaghten Memoranda, as it has become known. One, the final draft, is preserved in the police files. The other, seemingly a preliminary draft, was in the possession of Macnaghten's daughter, Lady Aberconway. The Aberconway version tells us that Kosminski was a Polish Jew, living in Whitechapel, who had become insane through indulging in 'solitary vices'. He had strong homicidal tendencies, hated women and was detained in an asylum 'about March 1889.' He strongly resembled an individual seen by a City Police officer near Mitre Square.

In the final draft, Machaghten adds that Kosminski specifically hated prostitutes and claims that there were many 'circumstances connected with this man which made him a strong suspect.'

So what we have here, on the surface at least, is a simple, straightforward story in which the top brass at Scotland Yard say that Kosminski was, at the very least, a gilt-edged suspect for these murders and in all likelihood was the perpetrator. Although, the point has to be made that, of his three suspects, Macnaghten apparently favoured Montague Druitt over him.

Serious research into Kosminski only commenced in the mid-1980s, through Ripper-expert Martin Fido. Martin ended up opting for a different suspect, Aaron Cohen, but what he discovered about Kosminski was invaluable.

He found that Kosminski had first been admitted to the Mile End Workhouse Infirmary on 12 July 1890, but was discharged three days later, into the care of his brother. However, on 7 February 1891 he was admitted to the Colney Hatch asylum. His age was recorded as twenty-six and his occupation as hairdresser. The form of his illness was described, simply, as 'mania', and his age at the time of the first attack – twenty-five – coincides with the six months duration of the illness given in the patients register.

But the admission book discloses a crucial difference on the latter point. Here, 'six months' has been crossed out and 'six years' was written in red ink. Immediately below it is another amendment. Against the words 'supposed cause', 'unknown' had originally been put, but then the words 'self abuse' were added, again in red ink.

Both corrections are of major importance. The length of time Kosminski had been ill in 1891, is crucial in assessing the case against him as Jack the Ripper; while the term 'self abuse' dovetails with the 'solitary vices' noted in the Macnaghten Memorandum. Both are euphemisms for masturbation – then thought to be a cause of insanity – and appear to pinpoint Aaron Kosminski as Macnaghten, Anderson and Swanson's Kosminski.

The Colney Hatch records also disclose the statements of the physician who certified Kosminski insane, and a lay witness. The physician, Dr E.H. Houchin, testified that Kosminski claimed to know the movements of all mankind and was guided by an instinct which controlled him. The instinct told him to refuse food and drink from others and eat out of the gutter.

The lay witness, a Jacob Cohen, endorsed this, adding that Kosminski had not worked for years and spent his days rambling around the streets, refusing to wash. He had threatened to kill his sister with a knife.

The illness Dr Houchin was disclosing is known today as paranoid schizophrenia; a condition in which the sufferer believes he or she can hear voices instructing them on how to behave. These aural hallucinations can also progress to becoming visual as well. Such, indeed, was to be Aaron Kosminski's fate, as noted in the records of the Leavesden home for imbeciles, to which he was transferred in 1894.

Contrary to popular misconception, paranoid schizophrenics are not necessarily violent. Only a minority are likely to be so. Most are simply the sad victims of mental illness, and that is what the statements of Dr Houchin, and Jacob Cohen, indicate. The written records of his stays both at Colney Hatch and Leavesden tend to confirm this. He was not violent, simply pathetic. The only instance of aggression attributed to him came during his stay at Colney Hatch, when he picked up a chair and threatened an attendant with it; but, given the sometimes brutal nature of nineteenth-century asylums, this might have been a gesture of self-defence.

Similarly, the only potentially violent act noted by the witnesses against him was his threatening his sister with a knife. A single instance of waving a knife around, during a heated domestic row, is hardly evidence of a violent persona. The asylum itself was plainly unimpressed, because the admission book notes that Kosminski was not considered dangerous to others.

These facts are all that we know about Aaron Kosminski. The Macnaghten Memorandum says that 'he had a great hatred of women with strong homicidal tendencies' (Aberconway draft), that these hatreds were specifically directed at prostitutes, and that 'there were many circumstances which made him a strong suspect' (final draft).

So, where is the evidence for this hatred of prostitutes, these homicidal tendencies? In this context, the crimes themselves cannot be used as substitutes to explain his motive. Instead, his motivation is supposed to explain why he committed the crimes. But there is nothing about Kosminski, that we know of, to suggest that he had homicidal inclinations towards anybody.

What are the 'circumstances' Macnaghten refers to? Presumably he is talking about the identification, but as we shall see this is fraught with difficulty and did not result in Kosminski's arrest anyway. The more one looks at Macnaghten's comments, the more one is reminded of the infamous 1980's political advert 'where's the beef?' Essentially, the problem is that there are large gaps in our knowledge, because around half the Scotland Yard files are missing today.

We move on to Anderson and Swanson's recollections – the 'Swanson Marginalia' as they have come to be known. What we find is a whole 'Pandora's Box' of questions.

We are told that Kosminski's family would not surrender him to gentile justice. There has always been a whiff of anti-semitism about the police's belief that the Ripper was Jewish. Anderson, in particular, never seems to have doubted it from day one. Yet it was based on little more than prejudice and 'little' may be putting it too high. In the 1880s the Jews were being demonised as alien hordes, taking British jobs and driving down living standards, in much the same way as immigrants are similarly pilloried today.

The cry went up and was echoed from street to alley and lodging house to tenement, that no Christian could do such things to women; the culprit had to be a Jew and a foreign one at that. The history of serial murder since reveals this to be abject nonsense. Archetypal Anglo-Saxon types, like Peter Sutcliffe and Ted Bundy, are far more representative of the genre.

Next, the identification. The 'seaside home' was the colloquial name given to the inaugural police convalescent home, opened in Brighton in March 1890. Why it was necessary to take the suspect and the witness all that way is unexplained, unless the police were terrified of the press getting wind of things. However, the date on which the home opened does tie in, very neatly, with what Swanson says about the aftermath of the identification, the records of the workhouse infirmary and the asylum. Kosminski could have been identified some time between March and July 1890, possibly during his July stay at the infirmary (Mile End subsequently became Stepney Workhouse), or shortly before February 1891, when he was finally sent to Colney Hatch.

So far, so good. But now the hob-goblins begin to appear. A former Lord Chief Justice has described eyewitness identification as 'the most serious chink in our legal armour'; and he is backed up by a conveyor belt of proven miscarriages of justice, emanating from faulty identifications. A battery of tests and experiments have, likewise, served to underline the frailty and flaws inherent in trying to recognise the person you saw, again. It all makes the point that, basically no identification can ever, by itself, be regarded as conclusive. And under what circumstances did Kosminski's identification take place? Was he represented by a solicitor? Was there a proper identity parade, consisting of other working-class Jews of a similar age, height, build and clothing? These are considered to be the minimum requirements for a fair ID parade.

Who was the witness? Two names are traditionally put into the frame: Israel Schwartz, the Hungarian immigrant, who observed Elizabeth Stride being assaulted some fifteen minutes before her body was found, and Joseph Lawende, who fifty minutes later saw Cathy Eddowes talking to a man in the passage leading to Mitre Square, where she was murdered. Neither would have been likely to fare well in court under a vigorous cross-examination. Both had briefly glimpsed a man in the darkness, eighteen months to two years earlier. Lawende had stated that he would not have been able to recognise the man again, whilst Schwartz's description of the man he had seen, plus the seeming anti-Semitic shout of 'Lipsky' directed at him (Schwartz), strongly implied that the man was Anglo-Saxon.

Other candidates for Anderson's witness include one of Lawende's companions that night, Joseph Levy, two unidentified men – who also, supposedly, observed Eddowes with a man in the precincts of Mitre Square – and an equally unidentified City Police officer, alleged by some to have been present that night. The latter is rather interesting. Macnaghten, if he can be relied upon, twice refers to this City Policeman in the Aberconway draft of his memoranda. First, 'No one ever saw the Whitechapel murderer (unless possibly it was the City PC who was on a beat near Mitre Square)'; and then again in his synopsis of Kosminski, 'This man in appearance strongly resembled the individual seen by the City PC near Mitre Square.'

This mysterious officer keeps on cropping up. Major Arthur Griffiths, crime historian and former Inspector of Prisons, was clearly afforded a look at the Aberconway draft.

In his 1898 book *Mysteries of Police and Crime*, he effectively repeats what Macnaghten said. George R. Sims, a journalist who most definitely did have good contacts at Scotland Yard, likewise refers to a Polish Jewish suspect in a 1907 magazine article: 'The policeman who got a glimpse of Jack in Mitre court (sic) said when sometime afterwards he saw the Pole that he was the height and build of the man he had seen on the night of the murder.'

Was Sims merely amplifying what Macnaghten/Griffiths had said in a literary form of Chinese whispers, or was he actually referring to the 'seaside home' identification? If so, then it sounds as though the identification was by no means conclusive; which faces us with yet another conundrum.

Was Anderson's witness actually the Will o' the Wisp police officer? As the Ripper saga unfolded, so the police began holding back evidence which might then trap the killer. Israel Schwartz may have been kept back from Liz Stride's inquest for this reason. Possibly, they persuaded the City police to do the same with their unnamed officer. In fact, it is just possible that some of PC Watkins' evidence was withheld, although it seems unlikely that he was Jewish. Their Ripper files were destroyed in the Blitz, so they cannot assist us. If the officer was convalescing at the seaside home in 1890, it would also help explain Kosminski being taken there. Likewise, it clarifies the surveillance on him being carried out by the City force, although here, in an offshoot to the riddle it is just faintly possible that Swanson was in error. Not for the first time either, as he twice mistakenly refers to Met Constable William Smith, who saw Stride with a man, as a 'City' policeman in a report to the Home office on 19 October 1888.

But the latter must be accounted very unlikely, as indeed must the whole thesis of a mystery police witness, tempting though it is. It is frankly unlikely that the City Police had any Jewish officers in 1888, and it is surely incomprehensible that any police officer, whatever his religion, would have refused to give evidence against a suspect.

There is however one alternative: he declined because he was not as certain in his identification as Anderson would have had us believe. This would also fit in with George R. Sims' article. His mystery policeman could only say that the suspect fitted the height and build of the

Robert Anderson. (Copyright Control)

52

man he had seen. Sir Robert Anderson was a man who believed what he wanted to believe, irrespective of what the facts actually were. In December 1888, he clung obstinately to his belief that Catherine Mylett had choked to death on her own vomit, when in the professional opinion of no less than five police surgeons, she had been murdered. Did he convince himself that the suspect had been positively identified, when he had not been?

The short answer is that we simply do not know. Possibly our unknown policeman from Mitre Square is nothing more than a mix-up with PC Smith from Berner Street. We really have no idea of who Anderson and Swanson's witness was. What thwarts us at every turn is the lack of hard information. That also applies to Anderson and Swanson's contention that their witness refused to testify against Kosminski. Here we have the most infamous series of murders in history– 'he completely beat me and every other police officer in London', wrote the City Police's Commissioner Major Henry Smith. Yet, we are asked to accept that that the police metaphorically shrugged their shoulders and stepped aside. Means of coercion were available and I really do not find this credible of belief.

To close the book on Aaron Kosminski, all that we definitely know about him is that he was a paranoid schizophrenic who spent over half his life lingering pitiably in the twilight world of the incurably insane – where he was considered to be neither violent nor dangerous. According to the correction made to the Colney Hatch records, in 1891, Kosminski had been insane for six years i.e. since 1885. It is arguable that, by 1888, he would have been too far gone to have exercised the control needed to have successfully accomplished these murders. Even if his madness was not then readily apparent, we are still asked to believe that the hideous voices in his head, ordering him to kill and mutilate, simply vanished and were replaced by more benign demons. Of course, there may be things in the missing police files which tell a very different story about Aaron Kosminski, but based on what we have to go on at the moment, the case against him must be held to be very fragile.

In fact, it is not inconceivable that Kosminski was confused with other insane Jewish suspects. One such was Hyam Hyams, who as we shall see was a most intriguing character. In April 1889, Hyams was confined in Colney Hatch after stabbing his wife. On another occasion, he had struck his mother on the head with a chopper, seriously wounding her. Hyams was delusional and also suffered from hereditary epilepsy and alcoholism. He was released on 30 August but ten days later he was back under restraint for good, after attacking his wife again. Known as the 'terror of the City of London police', Hyams was taken by them to an asylum in Kent, who later transferred him back to Colney Hatch, where he died in 1913.

The asylum records paint a portrait of Hyam Hyams as a frighteningly unstable individual, perhaps fuelled by a strain of insanity on his mother's side. Colney Hatch called him 'crafty and dangerous'. Often violent towards staff and patient inmates alike, he once attempted to cut the throat of a medical orderly with a knife fashioned from a piece of metal. Like Kosminski, he engaged in 'self abuse'.

Hyams fitted the description, given by Joseph Lawende, of the man seen with Catharine Eddowes. There are also some fairly startling circumstances linking Hyams with the events of 30 September 1888. Eddowes body was found outside the back window of No.8 Mitre Street, the premises where Hyams uncle, Lewis Levy, had once run a business. While Hyams' mother, Fanny Hyams was living at No.24 Mitre Street at the time of the murder, the same house where the wife of Lawende's companion, Joseph Levy, had lived as a child. Another of Hyams' uncles, John Levy (no relation to Joseph), was then resident at No.25 Whitechapel Road, next door to where the bloodstained knife was found on the steps, shortly after midnight on 1 October. Curiouser and curiouser!

The violence, the masturbation, and the time of Hyams' initial incarceration in Colney Hatch, match Macnaghten's Kosminski more than Kosminski does himself. But the fact remains that confusion or not, Kosminski's name must have been in the police's purview for his name to be there at all

The other possible suspect Kosminski could have been confused with was another Levy, Jacob, no known relative to any of the other Levys mentioned here, although both Jacob and Joseph were butchers operating from premises near to one another. In August 1890, Jacob was sent to the City of London asylum, suffering from general paralysis of the insane, the result of tertiary syphilis. He died there the following July. Insanity seems to have run in Jacob Levy's family; he had himself previously spent time in an asylum, in 1886. It has been suggested that Joseph Levy was really Anderson's witness and Jacob the suspect, thus Joseph declined to give evidence because he knew Jacob.

Whatever the truth, the City Police seem to have been watching a Ripper suspect who was eventually placed in an asylum. Inspector Robert Sagar, of the City detective force, is said to have written in his unpublished (and regrettably unavailable) memoirs, that they had surveyed a suspect who worked in Butchers Row, Aldgate, prior to his being incarcerated. This was not Kosminski because the suspect was working, plus Sagar wrote that he was confined in a private asylum. Moreover, Sagar said on a separate occasion that his suspect 'could not be identified.'

Was Sagar's suspect Hyam Hyams or Jacob Levy? Possibly; although the descriptions given do not, entirely, accord with either man.

Did Macnaghten confuse either Hyams or Levy with Kosminski? In Hyams' case it is conceivable. Macnaghten may also have had 'previous' in this connection. Author Douglas G. Browne, who was given special access to the police files in researching his 1956 book *The Rise of Scotland Yard,* wrote that, 'Sir Melville Macnaghten appears to identify the Ripper with the leader of a plot to assassinate Mr Balfour at the Irish office.' A possible confusion? The Macnaghten Memorandum does contain errors when he refers to Montague Druitt.

It is surely worth asking the question; if Anderson, Swanson and Macnaghten had not mentioned Kosminski by name, would we prefer him over Hyams or Levy as the suspect? Or for that matter Aaron Cohen, whose case is discussed elsewhere in this volume.

But they did name Kosminski and in doing so left us with the proverbial riddle within an enigma, within a mystery.

Bibliography

Begg, P., Fido, M. & Skinner, K., *The Jack the Ripper A –Z,* 4th edition, (John Blake Publishing, 2010)
Evans, S. & Skinner, K., *The Ultimate Jack the Ripper Sourcebook* (Robinson Publshing, 2000)
Fido, M., *The Crimes, Detection and Death of Jack the Ripper* (Weidenfield & Nicolson, 1987)
King, M., 'Hyam Hyams' in *Ripperologist Magazine,* #35 (2001)

Philip Marquis is a long standing member of The Whitechapel Society and its predecessor, the Cloak and Dagger Club. He comes from London's East End and now lives in Essex. He lectures on crime, and conducts walks on Jack the Ripper and other East End murders.

7

James Maybrick: Ripper Suspect

Chris Jones

James Maybrick (1838–1889) is the most controversial of all the Ripper suspects. He was a respected cotton merchant who, at the time of the murders, lived in Liverpool, the city of his birth and not London. He died in May 1889 and his wife, Florence, was convicted of his murder, although she was almost certainly innocent of the crime. James Maybrick was not considered a suspect at the time of the Ripper killings. He is not mentioned in the Macnaghten Memorandum, or any other contemporary police documents. Indeed, he was not linked to the killings until the emergence of the so-called Diary of Jack the Ripper in the 1990s. His credibility as a Ripper suspect is, therefore, intrinsically bound up with the authenticity of this document. In March 1992, Michael Barrett, a retired scrap metal dealer from Liverpool, telephoned Doreen Montgomery, a leading figure in the Rupert Crew Literacy Agency in London, and told her that he had Jack the Ripper's diary. The following month Barrett showed the diary to her and the author Shirley Harrison. It measured approximately 11in by 8½in. It was hardbound in black cloth, with black leather quarter binding and seven bands of gold foil across the 2in spine. It was originally a scrapbook or possibly a photograph album. The first forty-eight pages had been cut and torn out; there were sixty-three pages with handwriting on them and then there were seventeen blank pages at the end. The book provided a graphic account of the murder of seven women, including the prostitutes who are considered to be the five canonical Ripper victims. Technically, it wasn't really a diary at all. It had no dates and there were only a few references to family details. It is really a confessional document, in which the alleged murderer tries to rationalise and justify his terrible killing spree. It ends rather dramatically with the infamous signature, 'Yours truly, Jack the Ripper'.

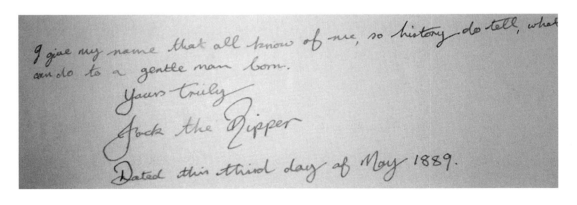

Extract taken from the Maybrick Diary. (© Robert Smith. Photo courtesy of Chris Jones)

Michael Barrett claimed that he had been given the diary by Tony Devereux, a retired compositor at the *Liverpool Echo*, whom Barrett occasionally drank with in the Saddle Inn in Kirkdale, Liverpool. He said that he had asked Devereux on many occasions where the book came from, but Devereux refused to answer his questions. In August 1991, Devereux died from a heart attack, so he was unable to substantiate the story. Since 1992, Barrett's account of how he acquired the diary has changed on a few occasions, including one version in 1994, in which he claimed that he had concocted it himself and had dictated it to his wife. To make matters even more confusing, Anne Graham (Barrett's wife's name following their divorce) has also provided a different account of the origins of the diary. She claimed that it had been passed to her by her father, and that she had given it to Devereux to give to her husband, whom she hoped would use it to write a novel. Her father, Billy Graham, would later say that he had been given it by his step-grandmother, Elizabeth Formby, who had supposedly been a friend of Nurse Yapp, who had worked at the Maybrick's house. Barrett now claims that his original story is the true version of events and that he did not forge the diary. He blames his changing accounts on the pressures of media intrusion and the breakdown of his marriage.

The debate over James Maybrick's credentials as Jack the Ripper took yet another twist with the emergence of the Maybrick watch, in 1993. It was a small engraved pocket watch, which had scratches on the inside cover of the case. Around the edge were scratched the initials of the five canonical Ripper victims; in the middle were the words, 'I am Jack'; and at the bottom was a signature, 'J. Maybrick'. To many, the watch was an even more obvious forgery than the diary, and even Shirley Harrison initially thought that it marked the 'first of the bandwagon riders', who would try to capitalise on the diary.[1] The owner of the watch was Albert Johnson. He said that he bought it for £225 from a jewellery shop in Merseyside, as an investment for his granddaughter, and that he only noticed the scratches at a later date. The watch has been scientifically tested twice; firstly, by Dr Turgoose of UMIST in 1993; and secondly, by Dr Wild of Bristol University, in 1994. Both experts agreed that the scratches were decades old and that it would have been extremely difficult for anyone to have forged them, and to have made them look old. One person who was convinced by the reports was the author and Ripperologist Paul Feldman. He came to believe that Albert Johnson had a Maybrick family connection, and that the watch had been in his family for many years. However, Johnson, who died in October 2008, never changed his account of how he obtained the watch. He always appeared an unlikely forger and his personal integrity was seemingly demonstrated by his willingness to have the watch scientifically tested. He even paid for the first tests out of his own pocket, something a forger would have been unlikely to have done.

A series of scientific tests have also been carried out on the paper and ink of the diary. Tests on the paper suggested that it did date from the Victorian era. However, tests on the ink produced contradictory results. Dr David Baxendale, of Document Evidence Ltd, concluded in July 1992 that the ink was not iron-based and this was significant, as he believed iron was a key constituent in all inks from that period. He later said that he had found a synthetic dye called nigrosine in the ink which had only been in use since the 1940s; thus the diary must have been written since 1945. Dr Baxendale's reports were undermined when Shirley Harrison found that nigrosine was commercially patented in 1867, and was in general use in writing inks, by the 1870s.[2] A second set of tests was carried out by Dr Nicholas Eastaugh, a specialist in dating old manuscripts. Using a proton microprobe to test samples of ink, he found the presence of iron and concluded that, 'the results of various analyses of ink and paper in the Diary performed so far have not given rise to any conflict with the date of 1888/9.'[3] However, he did add that it was possible that it could be a sophisticated modern forgery. A test conducted in 1994 by Analysis for Industry (AFI), for Melvin Harris, indicated the presence of a preservative called chloroacetamide, which was not produced commercially until 1972. However, the following month, tests conducted at Leeds University concluded that it was not present in the ink. Shirley Harrison later ascertained that chloroacetamide had been found in preparations dating from the 1850s.

The controversy over the results of the scientific tests, and the poor provenance of the diary, has led many people to simply dismiss it as a forgery. Philip Sugden has described it as a 'transparent hoax.'[4] However, some research seems to reinforce the view that James Maybrick is a credible candidate to be the Whitechapel murderer. For example, it has been established that Maybrick was a frequent visitor to London. Sir Charles Russell, Florence's counsel at her trial, said about James, 'You cannot follow closely the habits of a man who is in Liverpool, London, and other places going about his business.'[5] Professor Rubinstein has argued that the fact that all the Ripper killings took place at the weekend is very suggestive. Prostitutes walked the streets every night of the week; so why should someone want to commit murder at the weekend, when there were potentially more witnesses around? Rubinstein argues that such a pattern 'is consistent with the lifestyle of a Liverpool cotton broker who spent the weekdays at the Liverpool Cotton Exchange but was free to travel on weekends (as Maybrick was).'[6] Maybrick not only visited London frequently, he also had knowledge of the Whitechapel area. In 1858, he had moved to London to work in a shipbroking office. While there, he started a long-term relationship with a woman called Sarah Ann Robertson, who lived close to Whitechapel. The diarist wrote that he took a flat in Middlesex Street, in the heart of Whitechapel (though he provided no actual details that would have allowed this statement to have been fully verified).

David Canter, Professor of Investigative Psychology at Liverpool University, has argued that the location fits in perfectly with what we know about the 'activities and movements of many, but certainly not all, serial killers.'[7] We also know that Maybrick regularly used prostitutes. Mary Hogwood, a brothel-keeper in Norfolk, Virginia, stated that James frequented her brothel when he was in America. William T. Stead visited Liverpool in the early 1890s, to try to establish the truth about Florence's guilty verdict. He was scathing about Maybrick's character and wrote that he maintained 'relations with loose women'.[8] The diary has many references to arsenic and James Maybrick was a regular user of the drug. At Florence's trial, Edwin Heaton testified that Maybrick visited his chemist shop between 'two and five times a day' to drink a preparation that contained arsenic.[9] Dr Hopper, Maybrick's doctor, testified that between June and September 1888, he saw him 'perhaps twenty' times.[10] Sir Charles Russell stated that Maybrick 'had been ordered to Harrogate for his health' in 1888.[11] It was around this time, Florence told Dr Hopper that James was 'taking some very strong medicine which had a bad influence on him.' Therefore, at the time of the Ripper Murders, Maybrick's long-term addiction to arsenic was clearly having a detrimental affect on his health. Rubinstein argues that the reason why the Ripper stopped killing after 9 November 1888, was that on 19 November, Maybrick changed doctors and started seeing Dr Drysdale. He treated him, on at least five occasions, with homeopathic remedies and there was a gradual improvement in his health.

As research into the life of James Maybrick began to reveal that this outwardly respectable Victorian gentleman had a darker side to his character, other research unearthed details that supported the notion that the diary might be authentic. One example was the diarist's referral to himself as 'Sir Jim', on no fewer than thirty-three occasions. Maybrick's usage of this nickname was to be confirmed by an unpublished letter, written by Florence Aunspaugh and archived in the Trevor Christie Collection, which a modern forger would have been unlikely to have seen. Also, both Shirley Harrison and Paul Feldman have pointed to a composite sketch of the Ripper suspect that appeared in the *Daily Telegraph* on the 6 October 1888, and argued that it looks like Maybrick. Even more controversially, it has been suggested that there are bloodstained markings on the wall behind the mutilated body of Ripper victim Mary Kelly, that denote the letters 'FM', possibly standing for Florence Maybrick. Some have also suggested that the markings on her right lower leg are not random bloodstains, but the letters M A Y S. Donald Rumbelow totally refutes this view, writing that 'reading letters into the bloodstains is like reading faces in the clouds.'[12] Professor Rubinstein has focused attention on a letter that was published in the *Liverpool Echo*, in October 1888. The writer of the letter, who claimed to be Jack the Ripper, stated that he was about to sail to New York. He signed the letter: 'Yours Truly, Jack the Ripper DIEGO LAURENZ (Genuine).' Rubinstein wrote that this was the most important clue that we have about the identity of the killer. 'Diego' is Spanish for James, while 'Laurenz' is meant to rhyme with 'Florence'. Rubinstein wrote that the letter also explains the inexplicable gap of five weeks between the two murders on 30 September 1888, and the fifth killing on 9 November. Rubinstein also suggests that the very name, Jack the Ripper, could have been taken by Maybrick from the notorious High Rip Gang, who were active in Liverpool in the 1880s. In June 1888, a Liverpool newspaper carried a story about the gang's violent attack on a police constable, referring to them as 'high rippers'.[13] If James Maybrick was Jack the Ripper, he could have constructed the title by amalgamating words taken from the rippers and from the mythical figure Spring-Heeled Jack. The *Liverpool Citizen* makes it clear that, 'everyone' in Liverpool was talking about Spring-Heeled Jack in 1887.[14] The report even suggests that the character may have been a young 'buck', from the Cotton Exchange, where James Maybrick worked, who was acting in the manner of the mythical demon to win a bet.

Despite this evidence, the authenticity of the diary is undermined by certain key issues. First and foremost, there is not a clear line of provenance that can trace the diary back to James Maybrick. Secondly, there is a problem with the chronology of events. It is often assumed that the 'whore master' referred to in the diary, is Alfred Brierley, with whom Florence Maybrick had an intimate relationship. However, in a newspaper interview, Brierley stated that prior to November 1888, he and Florence were 'merely distant acquaintances.'[15] In other words, the Ripper killings took place before Florence's affair with Brierley, not after it. This view is supported by other eye-witnesses. Edwin Maybrick, James' brother, told Florence's mother, Baroness von Roques, when she arrived at Battlecrease after James' death, that Florence had only met Brierley 'this winter at some dances.'[16] The Baroness herself, in a letter to the Home Secretary in August 1892, wrote that in her early years of marriage, Florence was 'a delicate invalid, nursing little children, attending to the house...The December of 1888 was the first time during her married life she had been able to dance or had been out in society; and her health was then stronger.'[17] Another problem is that the Whitechapel Murders stopped in November, with the Mary Kelly killing, but James Maybrick lived for another six months. Is it possible to believe that the man who savagely killed Mary Kelly could have gone back to living a normal and respectable life?

Studies of the handwriting in the diary have also proved problematic for those who think it is genuine. The problem is, as Donald Rumbelow has written, 'the handwriting of the diary did not match the writing and signature on Maybrick's will or on his marriage certificate.'[18] Also, cleverly, the author of the diary provides no actual dates and is often very sketchy in his description of events. One possible reason for this is that the author is trying to avoid writing something that could later be shown to be inaccurate. Those who think that the diary is a modern forgery have argued that some of the words or phrases found in the document, simply did not exist in the late 1880s. An example of this was the term 'one-off', used by the diarist, which does not appear in dictionaries until the early twentieth century. However, research by Shirley Harrison found the term being used by a building company in Kent, in the 1860s.[19] William Beadle has argued that the style of writing in the diary appears to be 'more in tune with the twentieth century than the nineteenth.'[20] He believes that, while words and phrases that weren't in use in Victorian times have not been found, the diary lacks the over-elaborate style of writing that one would expect in a nineteenth-century journal. Caroline Morris disagreed with this view, and pointed out that the diarist consistently avoided modern contractions such as isn't and did tend to favour 'longwinded constructions' in the journal.[21]

The Ripper Murders could only have been committed by someone who was criminally insane, yet Maybrick was well-respected by his contemporaries. Even Sir Charles Russell, Florence Maybrick's counsel, described him as 'a man who seemed to have been liked by his friends and not without a kindly and generous nature.'[22] Maybrick's supposed motive for mass murder is that his wife was having an affair. If he really had been a murderer, then surely the first two people he would have killed would have been his wife and her lover. There are a few references in the diary that are either inaccurate, or have not been substantiated by research. One is the reference to the Poste House. The problem is that there is no record of any public house, in either Liverpool or London, having such a name in the 1880s. The

pub that is usually identified is the Poste House in Cumberland Street, Liverpool, but records show that it was known as The Muck Midden in 1888; it was not until the 1960s that it was given the name Poste House. The diarist refers to the Liverpool Cotton Exchange, but anyone who worked there, as Maybrick did, referred to it as the 'Change. Another problem is the reference to Mrs Hammersmith. As the woman had such a distinctive surname, she should have been easy to track down, but research has failed to identify her. Yet another issue is the diarist's use of the words 'tin match box empty'. The empty tin matchbox was not known to the general public until 1987, when a police list of Catherine Eddowes' possessions was

Letter extract taken from the Maybrick Diary.
(© Robert Smith)

first published. The wording in the diary is almost identical to the wording on the police list, published in 1987, suggesting, therefore, that the author of the diary was either really the Ripper, or he (or she) simply copied it from the list. Also, would the killer really have had the inclination or the time to have sorted through Eddowes' possessions, in the dark, and then have placed them all back in her pockets? There are also factual errors in the diary, concerning the death of the last Ripper victim, Mary Kelly. The diarist wrote that he cut her breasts off and 'left them on the table with some of the other stuff.' However, according to the police surgeon's report, the breasts had been left 'one under the head and the other by the right foot.'

Ripperologists have tried to produce a picture of the killer, from the thirteen or so people who possibly saw him. Philip Sugden writes that a study of the best of these witnesses suggests that the murderer was 'a white male of average or below average height in his twenties or thirties.'[23] Maybrick is, therefore, unlikely to have been Jack the Ripper, as he was in his late forties in 1888. William Beadle has argued that Maybrick was not only too old to be the killer, he also 'simply does not fit the psychological profile of a serial killer.'[24] He points to Maybrick's ability to interact with women, the fact that he had children, whom he appeared to love, and to the remorse shown by the diarist at the end of the journal, a concept he describes as alien to multicides. However, Dr David Forshaw, a specialist consultant in addiction, asked by Shirley Harrison to examine the diary, produced a lengthy report in which he concluded that, if you had to rely on the content of the diary, then 'on the balance of probabilities from a psychiatric perspective, it is authentic.'[25] David Canter, wrote:

> The diary may be a fake, but what it tells us certainly does not contradict what we know from other sources about James Maybrick, or Jack the Ripper. It also accords with what we can see about how a serial killer's inner narrative is reflected in the geography of his crimes.[26]

The diary, the watch and the circumstantial evidence surrounding James Maybrick, have convinced many that he was, indeed, Jack the Ripper. Although Maybrick lived in Liverpool, he often visited London and almost certainly knew the Whitechapel area. He was a regular user of prostitutes and a habitual user of dangerous drugs. In the summer of 1888, his health and demeanour were suffering as a result of his loose living and drug abuse. His business and personal life were in turmoil, and his wife was about to start (or maybe already was having) an adulterous affair. However, Maybrick will remain a highly controversial candidate to be Jack the Ripper, until the provenance of the diary can be successfully resolved. Paul Begg wrote, '...when faced with a possibly forged document the most important thing is provenance: the history or the lack of provenance altogether is highly suspicious. In fact poor provenance is alone sufficient to brand the diary a forgery.'[27] James Maybrick's coat of arms carried the legend *Tempus Omnia Revelat* (Time Reveals All). This is extremely apt because research into both James Maybrick and the diary has continued unabated, since 1992. For example, it has recently been discovered that Maybrick served on the Grand Jury in Liverpool, in December 1888.[28] The diarist, who continually ridicules the police for their failure to catch him, fails to record this event in the journal. If Maybrick had been the diarist, then surely he would have mentioned his time on the jury. Although this piece of evidence is suggestive, it is far from conclusive. Nevertheless, it is likely that in the future, research will unearth new evidence that will finally answer the question of whether, or not, James Maybrick was actually Jack the Ripper.

Endnotes

1. Harrison, S., *The Diary of Jack the Ripper* (Blake, 1998), p.239
2. Linder, S., Morris, C. & Skinner, K., *Ripper Diary – The Inside Story* (Sutton Publishing, 2003), pp.4–5.
3. *Ibid.*, p.18
4. Sugden, P., *The Complete History of Jack the Ripper* (Robinson, 2002), pp.10–11
5. Irving, H.B., *Trial of Mrs Maybrick* (William Hodge, 1927), p.179
6. Rubinstein, W.D., 'Hunt for Jack the Ripper', in *History Today*, # 50 (2000)
7. Canter, D., *Mapping Murder* (Virgin Books, 2003), p.94
8. Stead, W.T., 'Ought Mrs. Maybrick to be Tortured to Death? An Appeal from North America, and a Confession from South Africa', in the *Review of Reviews*, # VI (1892)
9. Irving, H.B., *Trial of Mrs Maybrick*, p.195
10. *Ibid.*, pp.32–33
11. *Ibid.*, p.69
12. Rumbelow, D., *The Complete Jack the Ripper* (Penguin, 2004), p.253
13. *Liverpool Weekly Mercury* (6 June 1888)
14. The *Liverpool Citizen* (29 October 1887)
15. The *Garston and Woolton Reporter* (17 August 1889)
16. MacDougall, A.W., *The Maybrick Case: A Treatise* (Bailliere Tydall & Cox, 1891), p.10
17. HO 144/1639/A50678D/99
18. Rumbelow, D., *The Complete Jack the Ripper*, p.252
19. Harrison, S., *The Diary of Jack the Ripper*, p.352
20. Beadle, W., 'Revisiting the Maybrick Diary', in the *Journal of The Whitechapel Society*, #20 (2008)
2. Morris, C., 'Response to Bill Beadle', in the *Journal of The Whitechapel Society*, #22 (2008)
22. Irving, H.B., *Trial of Mrs Maybrick*, p.231
23. Sugden, P., *The Complete History of Jack the Ripper*, p.367
24. Beadle, W., 'Revisiting the Maybrick Diary', p.15
25. Harrison, S., *The Diary of Jack the Ripper*, p.19
26. Canter, D., *Mapping Murder*, p.98
27. Begg, P., *Jack the Ripper: the Facts* (Robson Books, 2006), p.416
28. The *Liverpool Courier* (4 December 1888)

Bibliography

Books

Beadle, W., 'Revisiting the Maybrick Diary', in the *Journal of The Whitechapel Society*, #20 (2008)
Begg, P., *Jack the Ripper: The Facts* (Robson Books, 2006)
Canter, D., *Mapping Murder* (Virgin Books, 2003)
Harrison, S., *The Diary of Jack the Ripper* (Blake, 1998)
Irving, H.B., *Trial of Mrs Maybrick* (William Hodge, 1927)
Linder, S., Morris, C. & Skinner, K., *Ripper Diary – The Inside Story* (Sutton Publishing, 2003)
MacDougall, A.W., *The Maybrick Case: A Treatise* (Bailliere, Tyndall & Cox, 1891)
Rumbelow, D., *The Complete Jack the Ripper* (Penguin, 2004)
Sugden, P., *The Complete History of Jack the Ripper* (Robinson, 2002)

Newspapers & Journals

The *Garston and Woolton Reporter*
History Today
The *Journal of The Whitechapel Society*
The *Liverpool Citizen*
The *Liverpool Courier*
Liverpool Weekly Mercury
Review of Reviews

Chris Jones, a member of The Whitechapel Society, is a teacher and researcher who lives in Liverpool. In 2007, he organised 'The Trial of James Maybrick' at Liverpool Cricket Club – an event that was part of Liverpool's Capital of Culture celebrations. His book, *The Maybrick A to Z*, published in 2008, was well-received for its thoroughness and objectivity. Chris has come to be seen as an expert of James and Florence Maybrick, and he has given talks on the Maybricks in both Britain and America. His website: www.jamesmaybrick.org, has received more than half a million hits. Chris has continued his research into the Maybricks and, in the near future, he plans to publish a new book providing the definitive account of the life of James and Florence Maybrick.

8

Walter Sickert

Ian Porter

Walter Sickert's candidacy, as a Ripper suspect, arises from works by Jean Overton Fuller and Patricia Cornwell. Given that Cornwell's book, *Portrait of a Killer*, makes Sickert a high profile suspect, I will concentrate on this thesis. It has been widely dismissed due to its highly subjective, speculative nature, with poor research techniques used and clear mistakes made; roundly criticised not just within Ripperologist circles but by historians and art experts.[1] But the arguments against Cornwell are well documented and it would seem futile to go back over old ground. The Sickert argument centres round abstractions from pathology, art, psychology and graphology. The murders, and the time and place in which they occurred, seem secondary. I will take Sickert out of the realms of art and science, and attempt to place him within the reality of the mean streets of Whitechapel, in 1888. I will consider Cornwell's contention that Sickert used a network of secret studios, mastery of disguise and great knowledge of the local streets to avoid detection.

There appears to be a distinct geographical pattern to the murders. Buck's Row, Hanbury Street, Henriques Street and Miller's Court are equidistant from central Spitalfields. Profiling tells us that such a pattern killer often murders his first victim close to home, because he lacks confidence to kill further afield. So, whether or not one believes the George Yard murder was a Ripper killing, it does not, overly, alter the pattern. The Mitre Square murder appears to have been unplanned, the killer happening upon his victim by chance, as he made his way home from Dutfield's Yard. For those who believe Dutfield's Yard was not a Ripper killing, I still maintain Mitre Square was unplanned; soliciting the city being rigorously policed. Prostitutes, looking to attract city clientele, tended to advertise their wares outside St Botolph's Church, across the street from the city, in the jurisdiction of the Met Police. The killer would not have wasted his time looking for a victim within the City, and could not have believed his luck when he happened upon Catharine Eddowes.

The pattern indicates that the killer lived, or had a bolt-hole, in Spitalfields. So where does Walter Sickert fit into this pattern? Cornwell uses evidence from Sickert's friend, Marjorie Lilly, to state that Sickert had multiple studios in 'unknown' locations. This is confirmed by other friends, William Rothenstein and Ambrose McEvoy. Cornwell argues that Sickert's secret studios would have been well located as bases, from which to commit the murders, but there is no evidence to suggest Sickert had studios in the East End in 1888.

If Sickert enjoyed a network of secret East-End hideaways, he would have had numerous landlords. Such men built mini empires in single streets. Jack McCarthy, for example, Mary Kelly's and at one time Liz Stride's landlord, owned several properties in Dorset Street. Areas close to the murders tended to be divided along national or ethnic lines; some were almost exclusively English, while others were either Irish or Jewish. Landlords preferred not to rent to the 'wrong sort'. If Sickert had a network of studios close to all the murder sites, he would have had to rent from various landlords, who rented to differing categories of people. He may

Walter Sickert. (Photograph by George Charles
Beresford 1911, Copyright Control)

have looked out of place, needing to persuade
them against their normal judgement to
rent him a room. But perhaps Sickert used
disguise to present himself as a suitable
tenant, blending in to each environment.

Let us look at these surroundings and
the art of disguise to blend in. The Charles
Booth survey, 1889, reported there were
456,000 people living in Tower Hamlets. This
is larger than the area in which the murders
occurred, but Spitalfields and its environs
were the most overcrowded part of Tower
Hamlets[2], making up a good proportion of
that near-half-million population. But this is
the official figure. In reality, when a Booth
survey worker knocked on the door of a
tenement, or common lodging house, it's
unlikely this representative of officialdom
would have been given accurate information
by a landlord's bully, who had nothing to gain
from being honest. He would have distrusted
what the information might be used for, and
have a natural aversion to 'busy-bodies' poking their nose into his business. There must
have been inestimable numbers living within a square mile of the murders. And this was
a twenty-four-hour society; chandler's shops, forerunners of corner shops, were open
twenty-two hours a day (except Sundays), closing between 2 a.m. and 4 a.m. The homeless
who couldn't afford a place in a common lodging house (4d for a bed, 3d to share a bed and
a penny to 'sleep on the string' – leaning against a thick rope) were not allowed to sleep in
shop doorways; the police moved them on. They had to walk the streets all night, sleeping
in places like the graveyard of Christ Church, Spitalfields (nicknamed 'Itchy Park') during
the day. And people worked long hours; some went out to work early, others came home
late. The bodies of victims Tabram, Nichols and Chapman were discovered by people in the
early hours on their way to work; while the mutilation of Stride was interrupted by a man
finishing his day's work. Amongst the throng, there were an estimated 1,200 prostitutes
in the Whitechapel area at the start of the murders. There were sixty-two brothels, but
the majority of such women were streetwalkers, looking to service the rough trade with
a 'fourpenny kneetrembler' or a 'tuppenny upright'. The streets were full of unwashed
humanity at all hours. Jack the Ripper was not the unseen man portrayed in books and
films. He must have been seen by hundreds; seen but not noticed, unremembered, a man
amongst many, who just merged in.

Could Sickert have been such a man? The 'shabby genteel' appearance of the killer is oft
quoted. This could point to a gent like Sickert, attempting to dress down to blend in. But 'shabby
genteel' was simply an expression – the equivalent nowadays being that the man's clothes
'had seen better days'. More importantly Sickert looked nothing like the man, or men, seen by

eye witnesses with Annie Chapman, 'Long Liz' Stride[3] and Catharine Eddowes. But Cornwell counters that his normal appearance is irrelevant, because Sickert was a master of disguise, even suggesting he could have disguised his height. This all springs from the fact that Sickert was known to change his appearance by use of beards and moustaches; he also used different hairstyles and even shaved his head.[4] The one occasion in which this behaviour was caught, for all to see, was when Sickert wore an obviously false moustache in a portrait by Wilson Steer. The moustache wouldn't fool anyone. However, it is quite a leap to suggest that a flamboyant theatricality with his appearance makes Sickert a master of disguise, good enough to fool the world's greatest manhunt. This would seem the realm of Moriarty. Sickert didn't just have to fool victims, policemen on their beat and eye-witnesses; he also had to fool everyone he passed on the street. Every man was a potential suspect, and those who did not look or behave quite right would be the first to receive a backward glance. It would have taken more than ex-actor Sickert's knowledge of costume and make-up to transform him into the barely noticed man seen with the victims.

But there was a great deal of anti-Semitism in Whitechapel, in 1888, and there was a certain assumption by the local populace, fuelled by the hype of the newspapers, that the killer was Jewish. 'No Englishman could have committed such a crime', was one headline. The modern researcher has to be mindful of the prejudices of the people who have left supposed evidence. Could the eye witnesses have been looking for a Jew and therefore saw one? Was the dark hair reported actually the fairer hair of Sickert, disguised by nothing but prejudice and the black of night? Perhaps a disguise wasn't necessary when eye-witnesses often gave the police, and newspapers, inaccurate information.

There is, however, more to blending in unnoticed than mere physical appearance. To digress for a moment, at the start of Second World War, MI6 wanted to recruit British women who spoke perfect French to be spies in France. Few of those considered were used. The most subtle of English behaviour would give them away. Likewise, simply donning the clothes of a local man and using a disguise, does not transform a theatrical, young middle-class artist into a man who could roam the mean streets of Whitechapel unnoticed and unmolested. The area had numerous street gangs roaming around. One such gang had viciously murdered a

FOR GOD'S SAKE COME TO MY ASSISTANCE! — THERE'S MURDER! | AT THE CORNER OF HOUNDSDITCH | THE WHITECHAPEL MONSTER SEEN BY TWO MEN.

Images from the *Illustrated Police News*.

prostitute, just before the Jack the Ripper Murders started, and like all bullies they would have quickly spotted people who are a bit different. There's every chance that Sickert, attempting to pass through the Flower & Dean Street rookery – the most fearsome slum in London, full of bad men – would have been on the receiving end of violence, before he had a chance to perpetrate his own crimes. There were also vigilante groups on the march. If challenged by police or vigilantes, would Sickert, complete with disguise accoutrement and perhaps a false accent (he was good at voices)[5] have passed scrutiny?

We should consider how well Sickert would have known the streets by analysing the night of the 'double event', which shows the killer to have particularly good local knowledge. He managed to escape while pony and cart driver Louis Diemshulz went to get a candle. The obvious thing to do was to turn left out of Dutfield's Yard and head for home. The killer could be back in his Spitalfields bolt-hole in a few minutes. But he would have had to cross the well-lit Commercial Road and Whitechapel High Street to do so, and he knew his victim's body would be found within moments, followed by a policeman's whistle blasting into the night air. There would be every chance a man, making his way over those roads, would be seen and challenged by a Met policeman heading towards the whistle. But the killer appears to have had the presence of mind to turn right instead, and made for Backchurch Lane, disappearing into a dark, unlit netherworld of warehouses, railway cuttings and alleys; leaving the Met Police behind and quickly moving into the safer jurisdiction of the City Police, who would, as yet, be unaware a crime had been committed. Minutes later (the bodies of Stride and Eddowes were found just forty-three minutes apart) the killer pops up in Mitre Square, exactly where the route of someone wanting to make their way back to Spitalfields would take them – if they knew the streets like the back of their hand. Cornwell states, 'Sickert spent a fair amount of time in the East End and probably knew that run-down part of London better than the police did.'[6] Quite a claim. It is extremely unlikely that a non-local would have known the streets better than Sergeant William Thick et al. What is certain, is that the killer knew the streets well enough to make an astute getaway, despite the shock of near-capture and his desire to mutilate being tantalisingly unfulfilled, leaving his mind in what must have been even more turmoil than usual.

Cornwell doesn't consider the Backchurch Lane route. She believes the man seen by eye witness Mrs Mortimer, 'walking quickly toward Commercial Road'[7] after the murder, complete with shiny black Gladstone bag, was Sickert. Cornwell gets it wrong, Mrs Mortimer actually having seen a man make his way along Berner Street, from Commercial Road, prior to the murder.[8] According to Cornwell, Sickert made his escape by heading along Commercial Road (which becomes the equally well-lit Aldgate High Street), for fifteen minutes before arriving in Mitre Square. This is not the behaviour of a man who knew the streets better than the police. Having followed his near-nemesis, Diemshulz, and passing the club (in itself foolhardy), we are led to believe that, rather than scoot across Commercial Road, before disappearing quickly into the darkness of a street leading towards a Spitalfields studio, Sickert would have spent fifteen minutes walking along the best-lit road in the neighbourhood; knowing a policeman's whistle could be blown any moment. All this, whilst carrying what would have looked like a doctor's (and therefore suspicious) bag that, essentially, begged the next passing policeman to challenge him. But perhaps the one factor, on which all students of the Ripper crimes agree, is that the killer was lucky. He did arrive at Mitre Square, safe and sound.

Approximately ten minutes after he was seen speaking to Catharine Eddowes, by eye-witnesses, her body is found, throat cut and disembowelled; part of her womb and a kidney (which is particularly difficult to locate in the human body) were removed and taken away as trophies. What must have been about half way through those ten minutes, a policeman passed by Mitre Square, had a cursory glance into the square, saw nothing untoward and carried on his way. Policemen were required, by their conditions of work, to walk at a steady regulated pace, and their heavy boots, on cobbled streets, would have sent echoes around the tall buildings surrounding the dark, eerie square. The killer would have heard the policeman coming. For the second time in less than an hour, the killer stepped away from his victim, moved into the darkness and waited. By the time the body was found, the killer had gone. So the terrible mutilations must have been performed in well under ten minutes.

Did Sickert have anatomical knowledge? Did he use strangulation, purely because it was the quietest way to render his victims unconscious before slitting their throats? Or, did he knowingly kill them by strangulation, not just because it was quiet but because he knew stopping the heart would stop blood spurt? Cornwell suggests that a study of medical books would have been sufficient for Sickert to have gained whatever knowledge he needed. But the speed in which the killer mutilated, with the added hindrance of the darkness, suggests he may have had knife skills. The murders took place close to Aldgate's slaughterhouses, major employers in the area, and the knife used was something like a clasp-knife; the sort of jack-knife that a butcher in a slaughterhouse would possess. It folded back on itself and could be slipped into a coat pocket. No need for a shiny black Gladstone bag. Even the multi-talented Sickert did not have knife skills, and they were not something he could pick up from a tome on butchery. But there remains debate over whether, or not, the killer needed such knowledge and skills. Could Sickert have hacked away in crazed frenzy and come across the kidney by chance?

Given that Sickert allegedly made his getaway from Dutfield's Yard along Commercial Road, eventually heading into Mitre Square, he must have had one of his secret studios in the Houndsditch area of the city. But Cornwell states he also wrote the anti-Semitic Goulston Street graffiti. This means that, having got back safely inside his City studio, he then went back out on to the streets to do some 'whitewalling' as it was called in those days; chalking on the wall. Beneath his message about 'Juwes', he dropped a piece of Catharine's apron to tell the police it was the work of the killer. Sickert would have crossed Middlesex Street, which was the boundary of the City and Met Police forces. Perhaps he calculated the Met Police would be too busy investigating the murder at Dutfield's Yard for him to worry about them. But, before he got back into the Met, he would have crossed streets swarming with City Police responding to the news of another Ripper killing, this time in their jurisdiction. They were stopping every man they saw as a prospective suspect or witness.

Whether, or not, the killer left the graffiti is a moot point. It is the apron that is crucial. It effectively told the police that the killer made his way back towards the Flower & Dean Street area. It would seem one of two courses of events took place. One, it was a simple mistake by the killer. There was a standpipe close to where the apron was dropped. The killer could have washed his hands and wiped them on the apron, tossing it aside without thinking it would be a clue; the action of a man not thinking clearly, after killing two women within an hour and almost being caught both times. Two, the killer deliberately left a false clue to suggest the police should look for their man in the Flower & Dean Street area (Goulston Street was en-route between Mitre Square and Flower & Dean), after which, he doubled back down Wentworth Street. Either option suggests the killer was based in the Middlesex and Wentworth or Flower & Dean Street areas. It is difficult to believe the killer had a studio in Houndsditch. Sickert could have had another of his secret studios in say Flower & Dean Street, but if so, he would not have headed down Commercial Road in the first place.

The killer had started the evening by changing his *modus operandi*, going out to kill at midnight, on a Saturday night. The other murders, though at or close to the weekend, were not on a Saturday night, and were in the early hours. The killer clearly had a desire to kill that couldn't wait till the following evening. To go out at midnight on the busiest night of the week, when all the pubs were still in full swing, the chandler's shops were busy and there were still people going about their work, would seem foolhardy. But, if the killer was based in the market area of Spitalfields, killing at 4 a.m. on a Sunday morning would mean returning home when Middlesex, Goulston and Wentworth Streets were full of costermongers putting out their wares for Petticoat Lane market. The killer may have decided that killing earlier that night was the lesser of two evils (no pun intended). Better to be seen by a drunk, staggering out of pub at midnight, than the sharp eye of a costermonger a few hours later. But Sickert, the man with multiple studios, would not need to have worried about such things. He could have just used a studio away from the market. Come to think of it, why kill over in Berner Street if your nearest studio was a fifteen minute walk away in the city? With studios all over the place and so many prostitutes to choose from, why do the risky commute? But perhaps I am guilty of trying to use twenty-first-century logic to understand the movements of a nineteenth-century psychopath.

The killer stopped his carnage for six weeks after the double murder. Cornwell suggests the gap may have arisen from Sickert accompanying his wife to Ireland, throughout October, but there is no evidence he did so. The six-week gap in the killings saw London fogbound; none of the murders took place in the fog. It would seem more likely the killings stopped, because the murderer didn't like the idea of not having a quick escape route available. No killer is going to gingerly feel his way along the streets, because he can't see his hand in front of his face, in a 'pea-souper' fog. He could literally bump into a policeman.

Or was the journey to the East End simply too difficult in the fog? There is compelling (though not completely proven) evidence to suggest Sickert was in France at the time of the murders,[9] but Cornwell argues that even if he was, Sickert could have commuted between his base in Saint-Valery-en-Caux and Whitechapel to kill. But why not kill prostitutes in Dieppe, a town he knew well, which was only 20 miles from St Valery? Dieppe was a port, with many brothels (maisons de passe) and streetwalkers to service rough trade. Such was the demand for British prostitutes in French ports that there was nefarious procurement and white-slave-style trafficking of women, to open prison-like maisons, across the channel. Mary Kelly probably acquired her Marie Jeanette names from a stint in one. Cornwell argues Dieppe was too small a town, so it would have been too risky to kill there. But this fails to appreciate the compact nature of the area where the murders did occur. The planned murders were all within a few minutes' walk of Flower & Dean Street. Would someone with the overpowering desire to murder, of a 'habitual' killer, make the trek from St Valery[10] to Whitechapel before doing so? This is a killer so crazed he took outrageous risks which could easily have resulted in his capture; a man who killed Mary Ann Nichols on a policeman's beat with the PC just 50 yards away; and having killed Elizabeth Stride, was trapped at the back of Dutfield's Yard with no escape route, until the pony and cart driver went to get a candle. Yet minutes later he found himself again hiding in the darkness, feet from the body of another victim, whilst he waited in hope for a policeman to move on without seeing either him or the body. Would such a psychopath be willing to spend all day travelling whilst the blood lust was on him? I doubt he would have considered Dieppe too risky for his ventures.

I have treated Sickert as a *bona fide* suspect, by attempting to place him at the Ripper crime-scenes. But looking at the realities of Whitechapel in 1888, the case against Sickert falls apart. It would not have been as easy for a middle class artist to blend in to the hostile, alien environment of the East End, as Cornwell would have us believe. Sickert's alleged multiple studios do not equate to his meanderings on the night of the double murder, and he would not have had the local knowledge the killer possessed. It is probable the killer had abilities unknown to Sickert, and a crazed killer calmly doing a twelve-hour commute to kill is fanciful. Sickert should not be taken seriously as a Jack the Ripper candidate.

Cornwell claims to have been shown Miller's Court seventy-four years after Jack McCarthy's little slum was demolished.[11] I hope it will not take as long for the case against Sickert to be 'Case Closed'.

Endnotes

1. Example: Cornwell's interest in Sickert sprang from his paintings. He arguably painted works based on the bodies of Eddowes and Kelly. He did not paint his other alleged victims. Cornwell claims no photographs of these bodies were available to the public when Sickert painted them (1905–7). Photos of Eddowes and Kelly appeared in a book, *Vacher l'eventeur et les crimes sadiques*, published in France in 1899, whilst Sickert lived there.
2. Rule, F., *The Worst Street in London* (Ian Allan, 2008)
3. Liz Stride's nickname 'long' was not due to her face. It's cockney humour – long stride.
4. Jacques-Emile Blanche said his friend Sickert had a 'genius for camouflage in dress, in the fashion of wearing his hair and in his manner of speaking.'
5. *Ibid.*
6. Cornwell, P., *Portrait of a Killer: Jack the Ripper Case Closed* (Putnam, 2002), p.164
7. *Ibid.,* p.227
8. The police identified shiny black bag-man as innocent bystander Leon Goldstein.
9. Sickert's mother wrote from St Valery, 6 September, 'Walter and Bernhard talk and paint and both look and are very well.'
10. There was no direct train from St Valery to Dieppe. It took two and a half hours to journey the 20 miles.
11. *Portrait of a Killer: Jack the Ripper Case Closed*, p.12

Bibliogrpahy

Cornwell, P., *Portrait of a Killer: Jack the Ripper Case Closed* (Putnam, 2002)
Rule, F., *The Worst Street in London* (Ian Allan, 2008)

Ian Porter is an ex-journalist, novelist, guide and public-speaker. A Londoner, whose family was from Bermondsey and Limehouse, Ian wrote the novel *Whitechapel*, which is set in 1888. He is a public speaker on Victorian poverty and guides Jack the Ripper walks.

9

'Doctor' Francis Tumblety

Joe Chetcuti

From The *New York World*:

[Tumblety] used to explain his long absence at night, when he was prowling about the streets, by telling [his landlady] he had to go to a monastery to pray for his dear departed wife.

From The *Bucks County Gazette*:

[Tumblety] attended high mass at the cathedral, and was preceded to the service by a colored page in gorgeous livery, carrying a big prayer book in a velvet covered stand. This scandalized the worshippers and the 'doctor' was requested to worship less ostentatiously or go elsewhere.

From the doctor's ad in the *San Francisco Chronicle*:

[Tumblety] is one of the few mortals to whom the divine gift of healing seems to have descended as a legitimate inheritance.

From *A Sketch of the Life of the Gifted and World-Famed Physician*:

...I noted the fact that you were still engaged serving the Lord in a very proper manner – if such service does not bring reward in this world it must do so in the next. [Tumblety claimed he was the recipient of this letter from a physician friend.]

From the *Prince of Quacks*:

During December 1856, a patient, Adolphus Binkert, who was otherwise in good health, came to Tumblety with eruptions on his face. In the office, the doctor felt his pulse, shook his head and said, 'Poor fellow, it is all over with you and you must die very soon.' Tumblety told Binkert that he was in the last stages of consumption...At the time, Tumblety also gave him a lecture about God and the devil. In several subsequent visits, [Binkert] got additional medicine but the treatment did not seem to be working. When he asked the doctor about this, Tumblety asked his religion. Binkert was a Catholic and Tumblety told him that the medicine would not work unless he went to see a priest and got absolution.

From *A Sketch of the Life of the Gifted and World-Famed Physician*:

> While in Rome I had many cordial invitations from some of the most distinguished Princes of
> the Church...The highest honour I received during my sojourn in Rome was an invitation to
> visit the Vatican, where His Holiness, Pope Leo granted me an audience. On a former visit to
> Rome I had the honour of an interview with Pope Pius IX.

Francis Tumblety was not adverse to manipulating religion for the sake of his own benefit. He
often displayed letters he claimed he received from clergymen, but the authenticity of the
boast was quite disputable. His misuse of religion and misrepresentation of pious names were
tasteless acts of self-promotion. He even took this a step further, when a patient of his died
under suspicious circumstances in 1860. The doctor confidently invoked the name of a local
religious personage, in the hopes it would pave the way for his escape from legal trouble. The
short story deserves repeating.

The night before a coroner's jury, in St John, New Brunswick, declared him guilty of
manslaughter, Tumblety fled to the city's suspension bridge. When questioned by the
gatekeeper, the doctor smoothly lied, explaining he had been beckoned to cross the bridge so
he could come to the aid of a man of the cloth, one Revd Dunphy. In reality, Tumblety only
used that pretence for the purpose of safely fleeing from the city. From there he continued
on horseback over the American border thus becoming a fugitive of justice. His tale about
travelling to see Revd Dunphy was as fabricated as his excuse about travelling to a monastery
to pray.

As for his dealings with Adolphus Binkert, he cunningly used theology as a scare tactic
to recruit a potential patient. Having been raised a Catholic, Tumblety knew the basic
catechism of the Church and probably was aware of the fearful reverence the brethren held
for its canon, during the nineteenth century. The doctor twisted the meaning of the Sacrament
of Penance and used it as a means of persuasion against Binkert. He eventually victimised
Binkert to the point where he extorted a gold watch from the duped man. His manipulation of
religion became a convenience for him, while his successful exploitation of patients became
financially profitable.

It was said of Tumblety, 'He is not a doctor. A more arrant charlatan and quack never
fattened on the hopes and fears of afflicted humanity.' Throughout his medical career the
quack took advantage of the weakened disposition of ailing people and made vows to cure
them. Those empty promises often resulted in temporary popularity for him in numerous
cities. Needless to say, his days were numbered in each of those places, because the public
would eventually figure out the charade. When his patients realised they were getting taken,
things turned ugly. This was best explained in a letter sent to Washington DC by the Provost
Marshal General of Missouri:

> (Tumblety) has been compelled to leave several towns and cities in Canada for his rascality
> and trickery, and is being continually importuned and threatened by those he has deluded
> and swindled.[1]

Since there were no laws governing false medical ads in newspapers during his career, the
doctor used this medium, extensively, to misrepresent himself. Compulsory school attendance
laws began to appear in America during the 1852–60 period; first in Massachusetts and
then, soon afterward, in New York. Newspapers were read out loud in households on a

large scale. This national literacy development coincided with the growth of the doctor's ad campaign. Tumblety's arrogant display of big headlines attracted a number of gullible and afflicted people into his office. A key ingredient to his ads was the use of phoney testimonies from former patients.

The doctor's finagling of religion and tinkering of newspaper ads would not be needed when he desired to snare a young male adult. The force of his personality, along with the promise of continued employment, often sufficed in getting a naive lad under his control. As expected, these situations occasionally met with tribulation. The doctor's intimate involvement with his non-consenting secretary (a college boy named Lyons) led to court appearances in New York City. A similar type of problem popped up across the ocean. According to Detective William Pinkerton, Tumblety had to deal with the English police after he eloped to Liverpool with his teenage employee, Henry Carr. In addition, the *Evening Star* of Washington DC printed a letter of concern, because Tumblety was suspected of having run off with 'young Isaac Golliday' and neither had returned. Golliday and Carr each had a father who warned against sharing in Tumblety's company, but it was to no avail. The doctor had a reputation for sordid vice, and when he succumbed to it, an impressionable young man would get recruited. He continued to behave in a promiscuous manner even after the age of sixty.

Out of all his targets of exploitation, the armed forces may have been his favourite. He seemed to take plenty of pride when pretending to be associated with an army. There were occasions though, when this antic was not received well. One instance occurred in March 1865, when the doctor was arrested for dressing in military attire. 'Putting on foreign airs' was the charge, apparently. This habit of his started in the nation's capital, during the early days of the American Civil War. Pinkerton remarked:

> At that time my duties in Washington were connected with the secret service of the army and my attention was naturally drawn to [Tumblety] a good deal by his military appearance...A little inquiry soon showed that he had flooded the army with his handbills and with objectionable books, so much so that General McClellan issued strict orders that the circulation of these books in the army should be suppressed, on the ground that many of the books were calculated to debase the soldiers.[2]

It was understandable if the General had become annoyed with the man. A Rochester newspaper reported on how Tumblety would parade himself 'as one of General McClellan's staff at Washington. He was not on the staff, but dressed as near like an officer as he dare, and would follow the General's staff on horseback at a safe distance.'[3]

Tumblety later spoke of having been furnished with passes from McClellan that enabled him 'to go and come where and when [he] pleased.' The doctor kept feeding his ego, while openly disrespecting military decorum; inevitably, this had to come to an end. A highly-respected researcher in our field, Roger Palmer, has a newspaper clipping in his collection that told of a time when Tumblety stood before the Secretary of War, Edwin Stanton. The result was predictable, as seen here in *Brooklyn Standard Union*:

> Stanton, who was not as good-natured as the President, had [Tumblety] thrown out of his office one day, and, in fact, ordered him to leave Washington in twenty-four hours.

Many years later, Pinkerton informed a mid-west journalist that the doctor had indeed been run out of town. Stanton, however, may have had a serious reason to evict him. The National

Archives and Records Administration (NARA) has a handwritten testimony in its files, inked by a private in the Union Army. Tumblety was accused of selling bogus military discharge papers out of his medical office on Pennsylvania Avenue. The soldier named two men from his regiment who made this underhanded transaction with the doctor. It seems befitting of Tumblety that he would have taken advantage of homesick soldiers, but regardless, it was those deserters who bear much of the guilt in this matter. The NARA document is kept in a file pertaining to Edwin Stanton's successor, Lafayette C. Baker.[4]

After the war, his military theatrics continued. The doctor proudly presented a dubious letter of praise, written to him by General Ulysses S. Grant. He publicly shared personal correspondences, supposedly coming from Generals Robert E. Lee and William T. Sherman. According to the *New York World*, he appeared in Pittsburgh 'wearing the uniform of an officer of the United States Navy.' So, it was plain to see that his eviction from Washington did not cause him to change his ways. The charlatan liked what he was doing, and he arrogantly expanded his military masquerade act, with a European flair. The cover of his 1872 autobiography showed him decked out in a Prussian Army uniform. It was decorated with a variety of medals. After Paris was seized by the Prussians, Tumblety became fascinated by the French awards presented to physicians who had served in field hospitals during the conflict. The doctor coveted that type of an award, so he printed one up and placed it in his book. He bestowed himself with a Brittany Cross, along with a diploma for his devoted service to the Ambulance of Brittany 'in the qualification of Doctor during the war.'

Judging by his actions, one could say Tumblety had very little respect for authority, be it from the military or the Church. Even law-enforcement officers were treated with contempt. While in custody, during November 1888, Tumblety shot his mouth off against his jailers. *The Brooklyn Citizen* reported:

> Tumblety was arrested in London some weeks ago as the supposed Whitechapel murderer. Since his incarceration in prison he has boasted of how he had succeeded in baffling the police.[5]

Tim Riordan discovered a story about how a Pennsylvania police department received similar disrespect. This was in regards to Tumblety's antics in Philadelphia during the summer of 1863. The doctor had an innocent man arrested, and jailed, for allegedly

Dr Francis Tumblety.
(Courtesy of Roger Palmer)

DR. FRANCIS TUMBLETY.

stealing a gold medal from his medical office. The Philadelphia Police Chief blew his top at Tumblety, after it was learned the whole thing was a hoax. The doctor skipped town when perjury charges were brought against him.[6]

An unpleasant aspect of this study into Tumblety's life was reviewing the times he embarrassed the poor for his own esteem. A couple of reports showed he had developed a habit of randomly tossing money on the ground, as if he were feeding the pigeons. From 'Recollections of a Police Magistrate' in the *Canadian Magazine*:

> Looking at his hand full of [mixed coins] he said loudly, so that all the people in the shop might hear him, 'How did I ever get that trash in my pocket?' [Tumblety] picked the gold out in one hand and walked to the door and threw the handful of silver out the door, across the sidewalk on to the roadway, where there was a scramble for it.

From the *Brooklyn Standard Union*:

> The boys used to follow (Tumblety) for the money he scattered here and there...

A demonstration of his superficial benevolence to the poor occurred in Buffalo in 1859. The doctor announced he would distribute barrels of flour to the needy at a popular gathering site downtown. A local journalist from the *Buffalo Morning Express* witnessed the event:

> The crowd collected was very immense, and very little discretion was used in regard to the actual necessities of the poor. The whole thing, as our readers already know, was an advertising dodge, and reflects no credit on the originator.

It looked like Tumblety's distribution of flour fell under the old saying, 'There is no greater treason, then to do the right thing for the wrong reason.' His gestures of aiding the poor came across as artificial. By the same token, his self-serving behaviour transcended class levels. When the doctor began his career in Rochester, he obtained the signatures of prominent citizens in the community. At first glance, it seemed he was seeking respectable names to endorse his personal character. Soon afterwards the signers found themselves tricked. Tumblety took the signatures to Canada and claimed they were endorsements of his ability as a medical physician. He knew no boundaries when it came to taking advantage of others, regardless of their position in society.

So far, we have looked at the man's behaviour toward religion, pious names, physically inflicted people, newspaper ads, young male adults, the military, the police, the poor, and the prominent. All we have seen is a relentless manipulator with no scruples. For whatever reasons, some found this man to have been an entertaining showman. It can't be denied there were editors at the time, who enjoyed spoofing him in their columns (Thomas D'Arcy McGee was one, for instance). Roger Palmer explained it well when he publicly wrote, 'The 19th century press wrote him up as a buffoon because they had no other way of processing him.' Even today, there are people who admire Tumblety. They like reading about a man who boldly challenged authority and spoke up for himself. But, there are also those who loathe him for all the anguish he caused to others. You do not need to have a strong medical background, to figure out there was something seriously wrong about the man. To help pinpoint the disorder, we can turn to an item entitled 'Profile of the Sociopath'. Some notes and traits have been have taken from the work and are listed here:

Pathological Lying:

[Sociopaths have] no problem lying coolly and easily and it is almost impossible for them to be truthful on a consistent basis. They can create, and get caught up in, a complex belief about their own powers and abilities.

Grandiose Sense of Self

Glibness and Superficial Charm

Lack of Remorse, Shame or Guilt

A deep seated rage, which is split off and repressed, is at the core. Sociopaths do not see others around them as people, but only as targets and opportunities.

Incapacity for Love

Manipulative and Conning:

They never recognise the rights of others and see their self-serving behaviour as permissible. They appear to be charming yet are domineering. They may humiliate their victims.

Need for Stimulation

Shallow Emotions:

When they show what seems to be warmth, joy, love and compassion it is more feigned than experienced and serves an ulterior motive. Since they are not genuine, neither are their promises.

Promiscuous Sexual Behaviour / Infidelity

Callousness / Lack of Empathy:

Unable to empathise with the pain of their victims, having only contempt for others' feelings of distress and readily taking advantage of them.

Parasitic Lifestyle:

They tend to move around a lot.

Poor Behavioural Controls / Impulsive Nature

Irresponsibility / Unreliability

Not concerned about wrecking others' lives and dreams. Oblivious or indifferent to the devastation they cause. They do not accept blame themselves, but blame others, even for acts they obviously committed.

Criminal or Entrepreneurial Versatility:

They change their image as needed to avoid prosecution. They change their life story readily.

The notes presented here were not in any particular order, but they related well to the bullet points in the 'Profile of the Sociopath'. More information can be found in Caroline Konrad's study into the subject. Under the heading 'The Malignant Personality', she listed five features found in mentally ill people of this nature.

1. They are habitual liars.

2. They are egotistical to the point of narcissism. They really believe they are set apart from the rest of humanity by some special grace.

3. They scapegoat; they are incapable of either having the insight or willingness to accept responsibility for anything they do.

4. They are remorselessly vindictive when thwarted or exposed.

5. Genuine religious, moral, or other values play no part in their lives. They have no empathy for others and are capable of violence. Under older psychological terminology, they fall into the category of psychopath or sociopath, but unlike the typical psychopath, their behaviour is masked by a superficial social façade.

'Profile of the Sociopath' was influenced by the work of Professor Robert D. Hare of the University of British Columbia. Tumblety fell prey to those descriptions and can be identified with many if not all of them. His malignancy can also be detected in Caroline Konrad's evaluation.

Some of the most cowardly and horrendous acts of exploitation were the senseless murders of Whitechapel prostitutes, in the year 1888. From the list of suspects, only one name was drawn out and commented on by a former Scotland Yard Chief Inspector. The name was Tumblety, and ever since those words from John Littlechild have been made known, Ripperologists have debated over whether or not this manipulative doctor committed these unforgettable murders.

If ever the day should come when new evidence enables us to declare Francis Tumblety innocent of the Whitechapel atrocities, certain Ripperologists will experience a feeling of satisfaction. The most content Ripper historians might very well end up being those who rely on modern day criminal profiling techniques. Many use this popular system as a beacon in their search for Jack the Ripper. No light shines upon Tumblety when the profiling methods of today are superimposed on the East End of London, in 1888. As Roger Palmer once said, 'Tumblety runs 100 per cent counter to everything we are taught. Everything the Resslers are yelling from the roof-tops.'[7] Simply stated, after utilising offender profiling techniques, no student of this method will draw a conclusion about how a fifty-eight-year-old homosexual male killed and mutilated a handful of female prostitutes. Due mainly to his age and sexual preference, Tumblety does not come close to being linked with the current image designed for the Whitechapel fiend.

Conversely speaking, if evidence should arise resulting in a moral certainty to Tumblety's guilt in the Whitechapel Murders, then other Ripperologists would be satisfied; such as, those who respected the words of Inspector Walter Andrews, in December 1888, when he stated the Whitechapel murderer could be found among the current list of suspects. Tumblety was the best-known Ripper suspect in North America when Andrews came to Canada and shared his impressions.

John G. Littlechild. (Courtesy of Casebook.org)

Those who believed Inspector Andrews were not drawn in by the yellow journalism of the *New York Herald*. The pro-Irish newspaper wrote of how Andrews had come from England to engage in an illegal political enterprise. Some researchers simply did not buy into this. Instead, they sensed Andrews had voyaged across the Atlantic to gather information on the antecedents of Francis Tumblety; a task which was in accord with the Inspector's official duty of taking charge of the Whitechapel Murders investigation. This was a duty he shared with Inspectors Abberline and Moore.

As for the author, it is his belief that Tumblety was suspected as a Whitechapel murderer at a very early stage in the drama – as early as 7 August 1888, when the first East-End victim fell in George Yard. The suspicions against him did not arise from the police or the citizens of London. Instead, they came from a Royal Artillery Colonel who saw right through the phoney act his suspect engaged in. The officer took part in a military investigation of the George Yard murder, and revealed some of its details to the American press. The Colonel claimed his suspect was a phoney medical man and spiritually polluted. The correlation between Tumblety and the English Colonel, Sir Francis Charles Hughes-Hallett, is lengthy and requires its own chapter.

It is as true today as it was in 1888: those who understand Tumblety the best, are the ones who take him seriously. He was a Ripper suspect who was gripped by a lifelong malignant personality disorder. He was a manipulator of religion and a harmful exploiter of the vulnerable; a disturbed man who skilfully hit his targets without empathy.

Endnotes

1. National Archives, War Dept. records, File 'B', Doc. 261, JAO
2. Nobody has located any official record of McClellan having issued that order, yet it is true Tumblety had a history of peddling questionable medical pamphlets. He mainly sold them in Rochester and Canada during the 1850s. The literature was of a sexual nature.
3. *Rochester Union* (5 April 1881)
4. Document 1769, Turner-Baker Papers, Record Group 94, Records of the Adjutant General's Office, NARA
5. *Brooklyn Citizen* (23 November 1888). Discovered by Roger Palmer
6. Riordan, T., *Prince of Quacks: The Notorious Life of Dr. Francis Tumblety, Charlatan and Jack the Ripper Suspect* (McFarland, 2009), pp.96–7
7. Robert Ressler coined the term serial killer in the 1970s. While working for the FBI, he was credited for establishing the methods of offender profiling.

Bibliography

Riordan, T., *Prince of Quacks: The Notorious Life of Dr. Francis Tumblety, Charlatan and Jack the Ripper Suspect* (McFarland, 2009)

Tumblety, Dr F., *A Sketch of the Life of the Gifted and World-Famed Physician* (Brooklyn: Eagle Printing Company, 1889)

Tumblety, Dr F., *A Sketch of the Life of the Gifted and World-Famed Physician*, second edition (1893)

Evans, S.P. & Gainey, P., *Jack the Ripper: The First American Serial Killer* (Kadansha, 1998)

Other Sources

'Recollections of a Police Magistrate' in *Canadian Magazine*, Vol. 54 (Nov 1919–Apr 1920). Discovered by Stephen Ryder.

Brooklyn Citizen (Courtesy of Roger Palmer)

Brooklyn Standard Union (Courtesy of Roger Palmer)

Bucks County Gazette

Buffalo Morning Express (Courtesy of Tim Riordan)

Daily Inter Ocean (Chicago)

Evening Star (Washington)

Morning Freeman

The New York World

Rochester Union

San Francisco Chronicle

www.casebook.org

www.jtrforums.com

www.mcafee.cc

Acknowledgements

Appreciation goes to Roger Palmer for sharing the illustration of Francis Tumblety. Special thanks goes to John Spanek for assisting in the technical aspects of this report.

After twenty-two years in the medical profession, Joe Chetcuti retired in 2004. He has contributed numerous articles for two prominent London periodicals that deal with the Victorian era (The *Whitechapel Society Journal* and *Ripperologist*). Joe was born and raised in the San Francisco peninsula and still lives there. He is an active member of the Jack the Ripper Writers website. He is pleased with the growth of interest in the Martha Tabram murder case and senses that crime was a significant aspect of the Whitechapel mysteries.

10

Prince Albert Victor

M.W. Oldridge

Jack the Ripper was only the trade name, as he himself (or, more likely, someone ghostwriting his infernal letters) would have had it; but, from the very first, the day-to-day identity of the Whitechapel murderer was tantalisingly unknowable, occluded by the East End's trademark peasouper, or otherwise lost to sight in the Minoan maze of its bloody streets. The sensational *sangfroid* of the culprit thrilled and appalled – the killer wandered the streets unsuspected by the police, committed homicides of astonishing audacity, and fled again, all unseen. His work was an anonymous, effortless reflection on the horror of chance, anticipating the mad juxtapositions of the dreamworld, shortly to be mapped by Freud, and the accidental, abstract semantics of Dada and Surrealism. When the scare died down, all that remained of the Ripper was his cognomen, a Saussurean *signifiant* detached from its *signifié*, the chief symbol of his popular terror. Behind the soubriquet, however, he seemed to have abandoned his mission as invisibly as he had taken it up.

And so began the instinctive hunt for meaning. Out of the jigsaw pieces of his victims, the task of assembling the image of the Ripper commenced, haphazard, fumbling. The disjunction of this aimless mystery offended logic, and solutions were sought everywhere – the doctor bent on revenge, the sociopathic Russian agent, perhaps even the social reformer pushing the envelope of charity. And then, in 1962, with rival administrations on separate continents guaranteeing each other's destruction, with missiles hauling slowly, slowly towards Cuba, with the world never more than minutes away from ruin, another suspect was named – the one-time heir presumptive to the British throne.

Of course, every society gets the kind of conspiracy theories it deserves, but the identification of Prince Albert Victor with Jack the Ripper proved popular, informing Ripperology until the centenary of the murders. This anniversary was more-or-less coincident with the end of the Cold War and, with global nuclear efforts scaled back in the wake of the implosion of the Soviet Union, and with the setting back of the hands of the apocalyptic clock, there came a lifting of the paranoid burden. Prince Albert Victor dropped from the radar at the same time, his candidacy a monument to more fearful times, to the crooked potential of absolutism and imperialism, to the banished spectre of the annihilation of the masses by their leaders. Meaningful in its day, the Royal Ripper Theory was an unusual cultural victim of the political and social change of the late 1980s and early 1990s – like the systems it imitated, it became obsolete almost overnight, and was swept away, to be replaced by the information age, a generally untrammelled plurality of opinion, and widespread and remote digital access to data which were once much less readily available.

We are dealing with a relic, then; let us trace its provenance. Prince Albert Victor was born in 1864, the first son and natural heir of Albert Edward, Prince of Wales, and Alexandra, Princess of Wales; upon the death of Queen Victoria in 1901, Albert Edward would become King Edward VII. At the time of his birth, therefore, little Albert Victor was

Prince Albert Victor.
(Copyright Control)

second in line to the throne of the world's greatest empire, and it alarmed the establishment to discover, as they soon did, that he seemed generally to resist his tutors' attempts to educate him. He was perceived to be intellectually frigid, and the full range of disappointed, Gradgrindian adjectives was deployed to explain his lack of progress – listless, dull, dormant, the Prince made for a poor student. As a result, he was put to sea aboard the HMS *Bacchante*, returning to England three years later with, perhaps, a little more practical wisdom and, more certainly, a Japanese tattoo. He went up to Cambridge in spite of his apparent weaknesses, attending Trinity College, where, it is said, he was deferentially excused from having to run in the intellectual rat-race which went on around him.

This, however, is not to say that Eddy – as he was called by his family – had failed entirely to integrate into Cambridge's social whirl. On the contrary, rumours of sexual immorality and other unbefitting behaviour leaked back to the palace: while his intellect remained stubbornly undernourished, even in Trinity's hothouse learning environment, his libido and his capacity for drink seemed almost to have grown to compensate. Nature, then as now, abhorred a vacuum, but Eddy's concerned entourage were determined to map the sharp lines of discipline onto the virgin territory of his mercurial conscience. Another spell in the military ensued – Eddy chose his regiment, some said, because he liked the look of the uniform. His effete style bolstered allegations of homosexuality; his craning neck, impeccably waxed moustache and unusually long arms made him a curious physical specimen. This was the man who, theoretically, was one day to become King – when Eddy left Cambridge in 1885, his grandmother, the Queen, was well into her sixties, his father was in his forties, and the future of this aging monarchy appeared, startlingly, to rest in the hands of this impish, feminine gadabout.

Perhaps in spite of his own sexual preferences, concerted efforts were now made to find Eddy a wife whose strengths would lock, enzyme-like, into the erratic profile of his own weaknesses. Princess Mary of Teck was the lady identified, but, with the marriage only six weeks away, Eddy died at Sandringham, aged twenty-eight, on 14 January 1892. He had contracted a severe dose of influenza, which was then sweeping the court, and this led on into a fatal pneumonia. The grief of his much-tested family was genuine; shock was felt across the country, and transmitted by telegraph wire to the most far-flung parts of the empire; in London, Sir Edward Bradford, Commissioner of the Metropolitan Police, ordered his men into mourning, from which they would not emerge until 26 February. Elsewhere, colder – perhaps shrewder – assessments marked the elevation of Eddy's more capable brother George to the position of heir presumptive as 'a merciful act of providence'. Eddy's worrying peccadilloes no longer threatened to write themselves into the history of the monarchy and, were it not for the long memories of Ripperologists, he would have been very much forgotten.

But had the capital's police mourned a man whom, three and a half years earlier, they were desperate to apprehend? Was Eddy – in the moments between his bouts of drinking and, as rumour had it, his convulsions of homosexual debauchery – the greatest criminal of his generation, ripping female prostitutes to shreds on the dismal streets of Whitechapel? In 1962, Phillippe Jullien alleged that he was, acting, he said, in concert with the Duke of Bedford, a man who had died a year to the day before Eddy, shooting himself through the heart during a spell of madness. Little attention seems to have been paid to Jullien's allegation upon its publication, but, the other side of the Summer of Love, the dark charge against Eddy was laid for a second time. This time, the mouthpiece of the allegations was one Dr Thomas Stowell, a surgeon of Southampton, who published an article in the periodical *The Criminologist* hinting strongly at Eddy's guilt. Stowell had *faux*-discreetly attempted to protect his suspect's identity under the pseudonym of 'S', but the Devil was, as ever, discernible in the details.

Stowell's theory was, broadly, this: Eddy, he supposed, had contracted syphilis while on his global jaunt, and, in its tertiary phase, the disease had propelled the Prince into a murderous insanity. Creeping around the East End through the gruesome autumn months of 1888, he had been responsible for the whole sequence of Ripper killings, but Eddy found himself arrested shortly after the awful murder and disfigurement of Catherine Eddowes, and, under a veil of secrecy, he was sent to an asylum. From here he soon escaped, returning (rather daringly) to London for his *pièce de résistance*, the wholesale obliteration of Mary Jane Kelly. Recaptured and returned to the asylum, Eddy's subsequent care was delegated to Sir William Gull, the Queen's Physician-in-Ordinary. A man on the wrong side of a debilitating stroke, Gull was now asked to take up the most extraordinary of tasks: the rehabilitation of Jack the Ripper. In fact, he went about the job so competently that Eddy – shot to the moon, mentally, while his homicidal instincts held him in their thrall – was able to carry out perfunctory official duties over the next few years. Stowell, though, examining the matter in hindsight, detected telltale signs of physical and emotional deterioration in Eddy's shortening public speeches.

In addition, said Stowell, a carefully-managed smokescreen had kicked in. The establishment rattled out a disorienting battery of cover stories, offering false leads to the curious and red herrings to the rumourmonger. Behind the bluster, however, Stowell felt that he had seen the realm-threatening truth – and there were diaries, Gull's among them, which, he said, testified to Eddy's murders. These diaries, however, failed to manifest themselves quite as readily as Stowell may have liked – he had had connections once, and, metaphorically at least, the keys to the archive boxes of the Gull family (and to those of their co-medics and relations, the Aclands), but it appears that he relied chiefly on memory when he recalled Sir William's daughter referring to an episode in which the venerable Dr Gull told the future King Edward VII that his son, Eddy, was dying of syphilis of the brain. In Stowell's defence, he seems to have told a broadly similar story to the true crime writer Colin Wilson in the early 1960s – in retrospect, Wilson wondered whether Stowell had secretly wanted him to publish the tale. But perhaps Stowell was no better than partially reliable – when, in 1970, he finally came to place his article with *The Criminologist*, Stowell entitled it 'Jack the Ripper – A Solution?' The question mark may have represented the natural humility of a man aware that he had an astounding story to tell; on the other hand, the octogenarian Stowell may have found himself caught on the horns of doubt. Could he be certain? His recollection of the conversation with Caroline Acland, Gull's daughter, dated back, probably, to the 1930s.

After publication, it took almost no time to debunk the theory, but the episode was an irregular one, with, supposing that one was looking for them, potential conspiracy building quickly upon conspiracy. *The Times*, getting hold of the story in its edition of 4 November 1970, described the tale as a 'mischievous calumny', and reported that Buckingham Palace had decided to take the moral high ground, withholding its scorn for Stowell's revelations in a superior display of tight-lipped, royal disdain. The same article also noted that the newspaper's own records placed Eddy – free and apparently unsought by anyone – at Balmoral on 1 October 1888, a day after the murders of Elizabeth Stride and Catherine Eddowes.

Stowell responded to this knockback with admirable spirit, writing to the editor of *The Times* on 5 November 1970 to state that he had 'at no time associated His Royal Highness, the late Duke of Clarence [part of Eddy's official title from 1890 onwards] with the Whitechapel murderer.' Indeed, Stowell now wrote that he did not believe that the killer was royal at all – his opinion was, specifically, that the murderer was 'a scion of a noble family'. He therefore rejected the idea that Eddy's incontrovertible presence at Balmoral was fatal to his theory, and signed himself away with an artless, dactylic flourish, 'a loyalist and a Royalist'. This was game stuff, but the horse had very much bolted, and Stowell's retractions were untenable, absurd. It seemed as if he no longer wished to lie in the bed he had made for himself, but – strange to tell – he would not have to. By the time his letter was published on 9 November, Stowell was dead, and his papers on the case were swiftly destroyed. Had he said too much?

Notwithstanding the curious timing of these events, however, the manner of Stowell's death was uncontroversial; quite naturally, he was not silenced for his unusual claims, and, after his demise, Stowell's son, Eldon, burned his father's file on Jack the Ripper, having first checked that there was nothing inside it worth keeping. This act was lamented in some quarters, but Eldon professed himself uninterested in the mystery. He did not even seem to know – and less to care – why his father's name had recently been mentioned in connection with the Ripper. So Eldon was not, after all, a secret government agent conspiring to suppress his father's dangerous, state-breaking knowledge, but merely a son clearing out his deceased father's house. On an individual level, this was all perfectly unremarkable, if slightly sad.

Thomas Stowell's true legacy to Ripperology, however, would not disappear into the flames quite as quickly as did his file. For the next twenty years, give or take, the hunt for the Whitechapel murderer would be a merry-go-round of conspiracy, subterfuge, cover-up and misinformation, and, surprisingly often considering the *prima facie* problems of his candidacy, Eddy would be, however paradoxically, at the centre of the off-centre thought processes of Jack the Ripper's pursuers.

Prince Albert Victor. (Copyright Control)

In 1972, Michel Harrison, an author and Sherlock Holmes enthusiast, subjected the case against Eddy to further, book-length, scrutiny. In the manner of the subject of his passion, Harrison embarked on his enquiries fuelled by arch scepticism and Aristotelian logic – he was unable to access the official papers relating to Eddy's movements in the last months of 1888, but, working from other sources, he developed a vision of the Prince which saw him, now, not as the Ripper, but as the dull, probably unknowing, acolyte of the Ripper. Where Eddy had once stood, silhouetted against Whitechapel's dimly lamp-lit streets, Harrison now sketched in J.K. Stephen, a poet of ugly, misogynistic sentiment who had, in fact, tutored Eddy at Cambridge. A closer inspection of Harrison's reasoning, however, betrayed a flaw, a loophole through which Stowell's felonious re-invention of Eddy now tore, belying his biographer's attempts to exonerate him. Without the official documents to guide him through the period of the so-called canonical murders of 1888, Harrison was forced to assume that Eddy's demonstrable unavailability at the time of the killing of a *non*-canonical victim – Alice McKenzie, in 1889 – ruled him out, by extension, of complicity in the whole series of Ripper crimes. The Victorian police, though, had found it difficult to associate McKenzie's death with those of the previous year; they had postulated a separate assailant in her unRipperesque case, and so, in spite of Harrison's intentions, it appeared that Eddy was not yet rendered free from popular suspicion.

Eddy's candidacy had, by now, developed a rather peculiar form of resilience; the bubble of the Royal Ripper Theory had survived Harrison's attempts to puncture it, and, back in the world of Ripperological dreams, the mad urge to implicate the Prince simply grew stronger. Now, Eddy was up to everything and anything, some of it grounded in something resembling fact, some of it brazenly fictitious. His association with the Cleveland Street Scandal – an unedifying rent-boy saga, with Eddy playing a walk-on role, if the rumours were to be believed – put him into theoretical contact with all manner of rogues, but the allegations of his involvement may have arisen with the wholly unreliable solicitor, Arthur Newton, then attempting to wriggle out of (possibly trumped-up) charges of professional misconduct. Meanwhile, a more laid-back, mid-seventies interpretation of Eddy's sexuality suggested that he may, after all, have had an eye for the ladies, and another story emerged from questionable sources, this one describing an illicit marriage, an illegitimate child, the woozy mesmerism of Freemasonry, and a full-blown rearguard action on the part of the establishment. The crux of this revised Royal Conspiracy was that, in executing its grand, defensive plan, the establishment had apparently seen fit to tactically murder and mutilate a handful of Whitechapel prostitutes – fallen women who, counterintuitive though it may have seemed, were in possession of certain powder-keg information. The potential explosion was, once again, apparently big enough to bring down an empire.

This rendition of events pushed the aged, unwell Gull into the limelight. Stowell's theories had cast the doctor in a minor role, in *loco parentis* after the homicidal Eddy's apprehension. Now, he was reimagined as the killer, obeying Masonic imperatives (perhaps originating at government level with Lord Salisbury) to slaughter the small clutch of ladies of the night who knew not only that the wilful, hedonistic Eddy had married a common Catholic woman, Annie Elizabeth Crook, in 1885, but also that he had then had a daughter, Alice, by her, thereby rather upsetting the applecart of royal primogeniture. Mary Jane Kelly, Jack the Ripper's final victim, had, indeed, been a witness at the notorious wedding – or so the story went – and, when she realised that this placed her in a position of unlikely influence, she attempted to blackmail the government, suggesting that they buy her silence. Gull's murder spree was the establishment's brutal response to Kelly's impudent demands, and her associates went down with her, one by one: on reflection, it seems amazing that Mary Jane should have remained in Spitalfields, in her little one-room hovel off Dorset Street, assimilating the highly-publicised and extremely unpleasant serial assassinations of her friends and confidantes without, apparently, exhibiting much in the way of anxiety. Gull's un-Hippocratic mission terminated automatically with Kelly's murder, and, for good measure, the clues he had left at the scenes of the crimes had been packed with esoteric connotations, comprehensible only to the *cognoscenti* – the misspelled code-word 'Juwes', which jumped out from the enigmatic Goulston Street Graffito, for example, actually alluded to three key figures of Masonic lore, although it appeared at face value to be not much more than a semi-illiterate approximation of the word 'Jews', written on a doorjamb which happened to be positioned at the street-market heart of the East End's Jewish community. This was, all in all, an eccentric and somewhat charmless scheme, festooned with sideshow excitements, bit-part players and, lingering on the palate for some while afterwards, a powerful undertone of paranoid sensibility. Somewhere along the line, the trusty reputation-blackener which was the Cleveland Street Scandal found its way into the story, as did, for the first time, the artist Walter Sickert. Eddy's death scene now came with visibly-putrefying fingernails, this being, it was suggested, a sign of poisoning.

The detailed planning and execution which characterised this theory – given voice in the 1977 book by Stephen Knight, *Jack the Ripper: the Final Solution* – seemed on more sober reflection to have been excessive: it was overkill, to put it crudely. Supposing that Eddy had entered into marriage in 1885 (and of this there was no record whatsoever), then he had done so without Queen Victoria's permission, and in contravention of the Royal Marriages Act (1772). This made the marriage an illegal one, liable to immediate and unfussy cancellation, so there was very little here – legally speaking – which merited the concoction of an elaborate multiple-murder plan by the establishment, supposedly running scared. The story was off-wavelength in other ways, too, and there is evidence to suggest that Knight himself knew that the foundations of his solution were, in fact, terribly shaky. A solid debunking of this second-generation Royal Conspiracy theory did not prevent its being taken into the public consciousness, however, and Ripperology's fantasists, all starting from Knight's cynical headspace, maintained their grip on the discipline for another decade.

Times gradually changed, however. *Glasnost* and *perestroika* altered the face of Ripper studies as the centenary of the crimes approached, and, with crabby old conspiracy theories quickly shedding their relevance, so Eddy's star inevitably faded. There was one last hurrah, which came in 1991 in the form of Melvyn Fairclough's *The Ripper and the Royals*, a portmanteau of ambitious plots and manoeuvrings in which a raving Eddy lived on, incarcerated among the ghosts of Glamis Castle, into the 1930s. Fairclough's book belonged naturally to an era which had already passed without ceremony, however – the author himself repudiated his story a few years after its publication.

In this way, Eddy was, finally, permitted to step down from Ripperology's first rank. He had been an unlikely figurehead in frightened times, but he jarred with the discipline's democratisation, and he showed his age. Stowell's enthusiasm had come to nothing; Knight's visions had blurred; both men were dead. Fairclough's abandonment of Eddy's platform brought the era of royal intrigue to a forlorn end, and nothing seems likely, now, to revive responsible interest in a theory which, eventually, failed to adapt to its changing environment. The marginalisation of the idea's central figure inevitably followed.

And so Eddy's right out there on the horizon now, and his stock is lower than ever, but his hands are quite unbound and his curious little eyes twinkle back at us. And, below the perfectly-kept moustache, that's a smile, and the taste of *crème de menthe* on his lips.

M.W. Oldridge is the author of *Murder and Crime – Whitechapel and District*, published by The History Press. He lives in London and is a member of The Whitechapel Society. He has contributed articles to The *Whitechapel Society Journal* and is currently proof-reading for *Casebook Examiner*.

11

Suspects: The Best (or Worst) of the Rest

William Beadle

Jack the Ripper was not the world's first serial killer. Gesina Gottfried in Germany; Helene Jegado, Charles Avinmain and Eusebus Pieydagnelle in France; Italy's Vincenz Vezeni and Americans Jane Toppan and Jesse Pomeroy all preceded him. In fact, it is arguable whether Jack was even East London's first serial homicide. 'A murderer who is such by passion and by wolfish craving for bloodshed as a mode of unnatural luxury cannot relapse into inertia,' wrote Thomas De Quincey in his 1827 dissertation on the Ratcliffe Highway murders of December 1811; in which two families were butchered just south of where the Ripper later killed Elizabeth Stride. Note the prescience of De Qunicey's words; he not only foretells what is to come but also describes what these human werewolves are; men and women who kill for sexual pleasure, pure sadism, fame megalomania, a messianic purpose or vengeance against a gender or group of people.

But the Ratcliffe Highway murders had been largely forgotten when the Ripper emerged onto the same stage, seventy-seven years later. What distinguished him from those who had gone before is that his crimes coincided with the growth of the tabloid press, which requires a constant infusion of sensational stories in order to sell their wares. Thus Jack the Ripper became the first serial killer to be widely publicised: '...as each murder was committed we wrote up picturesque and lurid details...one evening Springfield would publish a theory, next night Charley Hands would have a far better one and then I would weigh in with another theory in the Globe,' recalled the journalist William Le Queux. It was Le Queux, and his ilk, who made the Ripper what he is today; the symbol of silent butchery the world over, as he stalks the gaslit streets of East London, cutting down one prostitute after another, a demonic force erupting out of the fog with all the fury of Hades.

Images from the *Illustrated Police News.*

The reality is that Jack never struck on a foggy night and the eruptions were very likely fuelled by alcohol; an estimated 68 per cent of serial killers have drink or drug problems. Lost in a fast shuffle were the victims – a group of women subsisting amongst the poorest of the poor of Whitechapel and Spitalfields – 'who [had] no home except the kitchen of a low lodging house; to sit there, sick and weak, bruised and wretched; to be turned out after midnight to earn the requisite pence, anywhere and anyhow; to come across your murderer and caress your assassin,' said the *Daily Telegraph*, in one of the few pieces of decent journalism marking these murders. It was the victims' so-called betters, the upper classes of Britain, who created the parlour game of 'name the Ripper'. By doing so, they diverted attention away from the conditions of which the *Daily Telegraph* complained and made common cause with the mythmakers.

Such is the aura that has been created around these crimes, that people seem to believe that Jack the Ripper walked between the raindrops, leaving the cream of two police forces floundering in his wake. In the eyes of the mythologists, he cannot, therefore, have been any ordinary person. So, it is no surprise that in the era of Watergate he spawned his own grand conspiracy theory, one which over a twenty-year period dragged into its purview a representative selection of the British ruling class of the late nineteenth century: Prime Minister Salisbury, Police Commissioner Sir Charles Warren and his Chief of Detectives Sir Robert Anderson, the Duke of Marlborough, Lord Randolph Churchill, Lord Euston, Lord Arthur Somerset, James Kenneth Stephen (the son of an eminent Judge), Sir William Gull, Physician-in-Ordinary to the Queen, the artist Walter Sickert and last, but oh-so-certainly not the least, Prince Edward Victor, Duke of Clarence and Avondale, heir presumptive to the throne. Peering through the curtains is the future King George V and, in a variant on the story, his Father Edward VII, then Prince of Wales, is involved.

I have left it to my colleagues to examine for you the individual cases of Gull, Sickert and Prince Eddy, along with those of seven other candidates who have merited their own individual chapters. In this particular essay I will be concentrating on four men, who, likewise, have received their share of attention as possible Rippers: the aforementioned James Stephen, Robert Donston Stephenson, Aaron Davis Cohen and George Hutchinson.

Stephen was inducted into the lexicon of Ripper suspects by author Michael Harrison, in 1972. The purpose of Harrison's book was to debunk the case against the Duke of Clarence: '...I couldn't leave the reader high and dry so what I did was find somebody I thought was a likely candidate,' he told the BBC. There are good Ripper suspects and there are bad Ripper suspects (the majority), but Mr Harrison is surely unique in accusing somebody simply to entertain an audience. A man's posthumous reputation was clearly of no concern to him, as he crumbled Jim Stephen's good name to pieces in the palms of his hands. Unhappily, in Harrison's wake, along came a number of other writers to spin Stephen into their own pet theories: he and Clarence had committed the murders together, or he supported and succoured the Prince while he carried them out, or he was part of a plot to cover up the birth of an illegitimate royal baby – one fathered by Clarence – alternatively one sired by the future King Edward VII (see above). It is all rather like seeing a man put into the stocks and watching him being pelted with rotten fruit and eggs.

There is not even the ghost of a semblance of a fact to link James Stephen with the Jack the Ripper Murders, and he fails the profile of the killer prepared by the FBI's experts in the 1980s almost completely.

Born in 1859, a scion of the powerful Stephen family, the inordinately handsome James Kenneth was a Cambridge don at twenty-six, president of the Cambridge Union and tutor and friend to the Duke of Clarence. He published two books of poetry and on leaving university became a barrister. A brilliant orator with a magnetic personality, success seemed to stretch out almost endlessly before him. Then it all went horribly wrong. In 1886, he suffered brain damage in an accident and from then on it was all downhill. His behaviour became increasingly erratic and in 1892 he died in a Northamptonshire mental home.

A tragic end to a young and promising life and there is no reason to suppose that during his decline he took to the streets to murder poor women in the night or connive in their butchery. He exhibited no signs of violent behaviour, matches no description of the killer and had no known knowledge of the streets and alleys of Whitechapel. He may have been a misogynist; it is possible to infer such from some of his poetry. He was indeed a close friend of the young Prince Eddy and may have been gay. It is even plausible that the two men were slightly more than friends. So what? These are no more the criteria for a serial murderer than any other lifestyle.

Michael Harrison believed that Stephen was acting out a poem called 'Kaphoozelum'. Or rather he wasn't because the actual poem is innocuous. However, the name itself is derived from a piece of doggerel about the murders of ten prostitutes in ancient Jerusalem. But why then were there not ten Ripper victims? Oh but there were said Mr Harrison. To Smith, Tabram, Nichols, Chapman, Stride, Eddowes and Kelly, he added four fringe victims: Annie Farmer and Rose Mylett (November and December 1888), Alice Mackenzie (1889) and Frances Coles (1891). But that makes eleven. No sweat; Harrison counted Stride and Eddowes as one as they were on the same night. Facts! It is very unlikely that Smith, Mylett, Mackenzie and Coles were Ripper victims, and Annie Farmer definitely not. She wasn't even murdered; she suffered a minor injury to the throat, possibly self inflicted, whilst attempting to bilk a client. Not exactly meticulous research but it perhaps sums up Michael Harrison's approach.

He also thought it significant that these eleven, sorry ten, crimes took place during university vacations or half-term holidays. Specious might be a better word. They would only become important if there was some good reason to think that Stephen had committed the crimes in the first place, and there isn't. If the wellspring of the case against him is bone dry, then all the derivatives fall too, because there is nothing tangible on which they can be based.

Our next suspect, Robert Donston Stephenson, is, I am afraid, not much better. According to his proponent, the late Melvin Harris, the killer was a black magician who was seeking to obtain the skin of a suicide, nails from a murderer's gallows, candles made from human fat and a preparation concocted from certain portions of the bodies of prostitutes, whose murders had to take place on sites which, taken together, formed a cross on the map. Stephenson, allegedly a black magician of great drive and determination, who had vanquished witch doctors in Africa, set out to achieve this.

Well of course he didn't. Stephenson was no more Jack the Ripper than I am; or a black magician, or any of the myriad creatures of daring-do, who visited him at the bottom of a glass. But once again, we can see that people want to see the Ripper as someone extraordinary, even if in this instance the only thing out of the ordinary about the suspect is his fantasies. Now, of course, deviant fantasies are signposts in the development of a serial killer and they are often heavy drinkers too, but in Stephenson's case, they point to a man who was merely pathetic and lived in his imagination the life he was unable to live in reality. Many people do, but most do not actively pretend to be the hero of their daydreams.

Stephenson was born in Hull, in 1841, which would make him forty-seven in 1888, rather old for a serial killer to erupt; rather older too than the man described by witnesses as being in the company of Chapman, Stride, Eddowes and Kelly, shortly before their murders. Although neither point is actually decisive, they do mount up.

The evidence is that, up to 1868, Stephenson was either unemployed and living with his parents, or working as a Customs Officer in Hull. His own, much more fanciful account of his life has him studying chemistry, medicine and the occult in western Europe, campaigning with Garibaldi in Italy, as a surgeon, and combating black magic in Cameroon. At best, none of this can be factually established and at worst some, Cameroon for instance, is provably false. In 1868, he was discharged by the Customs for living what they termed 'an immoral life'. Their records state that he had also been suffering from 'brain fever', meaning meningitis (I prefer the original definition!).

Judging from what scanty records there are, Stephenson seems to have spent the next twenty years living a hum-drum life in London, which included getting married and changing his name to Roslyn D'Onston. He claimed to have prospected for gold in California, including killing a man for seducing his cousin's girlfriend and seeking the Indian rope trick in India. There is anecdotal testimony that he may actually have visited India. At some point along the line, he appears to have divested himself of his wife. Precisely how he maintained himself is unclear, but he does seem to have scraped a living of sorts as a freelance journalist.

July 1888 finds him in the London hospital, Whitechapel, being treated for neurasthenia. The proximity of the hospital to the murders has led to speculation that he could have crept out at night to commit the murders, but his incarceration there obviously has equal weight as an alibi. Specifically, the ward he was in was apparently one which was locked up at night. On 26 December 1888, Stephenson visited Scotland Yard to voice his suspicions that the Ripper was a doctor at the hospital, named Morgan Davies. A surviving document indicates that Stephenson was motivated by the reward money on offer for the killer's conviction. The detective who interviewed him, an Inspector Roots, knew Stephenson personally and portrayed him to his superiors as a virtual alcoholic; it figures. In fact, earlier that month Stephenson had persuaded the *Pall Mall Gazette* to publish an article on the Ripper Murders, entitled 'Who is the Whitechapel Demon (by one who thinks he knows)', in which he outlined his black magic theory. This is alleged to have been a veiled confession to the murders, fulfilling his need to tell the world what he had done and why, with his subsequent accusations against Dr Davies a cunning ploy to divert attention away from himself. Others may think that drink money was a more feasible imperative.

But this is not the end of the story. The year 1890 found Stephenson/D'Onston living with a female writer named Mabel Collins. Collins wrote to her friend (and former lover) Baroness Vittoria Cremers, '[He is] a great magician who has wonderful magical secrets.' He was also now passing himself off as a Cavalry officer. Cremers eventually moved in with them and the trio opened up a cosmetics business.

Years later, in the 1920s, Cremers said that she had found a number of ties encrusted with dried blood in a trunk in Stephenson's room, claiming that he had repeated his story of Davies being the Ripper, adding that the Doctor had concealed the organs he had removed from the victims between his shirt and tie.

Ultimately Mabel and Stephenson split up. There seems little doubt that the Baroness engineered this to get Collins back, by using Stephenson's Ripper fictions against him, inventing the story of finding the ties to make her frightened of him.

The last known act of Stephenson's life was the publication of a religious work called *The Patristic Gospels* in 1904. When and how he died is unknown.

There is no real case against Robert Stephenson, aka Roslyn D'Onston, as Jack the Ripper. When one peers carefully behind the black magician façade, the real self-image is of a man who yearned to be a hero, actually defeating black magic, not a sadistic serial killer, cutting a swathe through the female population. He had normal relations with women and would not simply have ceased killing and settled back into domesticity after 1888, if he had been the Ripper.

The case of Aaron Davis (or David) Cohen is much more straightforward. He was arrested in the East End on 6 December 1888, as a 'lunatic wandering at large'. Details are not plentiful, but he may have behaved in some deranged way in a brothel. Such may be inferred from court documents on the 7th. Thames Magistrates Court referred Cohen to the Whitechapel Workhouse Infirmary for observation and on the 21 December he was committed to Colney Hatch lunatic asylum. He died there on 20 October 1889, from 'exhaustion of mania and pulmonary phthisis'/

According to the assessments of both institutions, Cohen was 'suicidal, dangerous to others, very violent, continually spitting and tore down a lead pipe and window guard in the ward [infirmary]; tore his clothes, kicked passers-by, was highly excitable, unclean, incoherent and rambling and required constant supervision [asylum].'

Initially, it was very difficult to get him to take food, which accounted for him being 'exceedingly thin' (Colney Hatch).

In the records, Cohen is described as a 'Tailor...a young foreign Jew with dark brown eyes.' One assumes that he himself provided the authorities with his name and occupation as the asylum's casebook lists his relatives as 'unknown'.

It has to be said that Cohen, brought to the fore by Ripper-expert Martin Fido in the 1980s, is a viable suspect. He was apprehended a month after the murder of Mary Kelly and, discounting Mylett, Mackenzie and Coles as Ripper victims (virtually all writers do), the murders ceased after his incarceration, at least in London. Cohen fits the basic profile, FBI expert John Douglas remarking that the killer would either have been Cohen or somebody like him. His behaviour and demeanour were violent and he may have posed a threat to the females in the brothel, in which he was apparently arrested. Martin Fido consulted Dr Luigi Cancrini, Professor of Psychology at the University of Bologna, who had given a paper on the Ripper's psychopathology. Dr Cancrini told him that Cohen and his behaviour fitted his reading of the murderer.

These are the pros and they are weighty ones. But there is also one major con, laid out for us by Dr P.T. d'Orban, Consultant Psychiatrist at the Royal Free Hospital, who remarks that Cohen's extreme mania would have undermined the control needed to commit the murders and get away afterwards. This echoes a point made in my 1995 work *Jack the Ripper: Anatomy of a Myth*, in which I describe Cohen as too obviously a lunatic.

Our final candidate is an unemployed labourer named George Hutchinson. Research, although taken very painstakingly by his advocates, has not conclusively pinpointed him. Ripper expert Bob Hinton believes that he was the George Hutchinson born in Shadwell, East London, in December 1859; the son of a licensed victualler. Hutchinson is listed as a barman working in a pub in Clerkenwell in the 1881 census. By 1888, he was unemployed and living in the Victoria Working Men's Home, Commercial Street, Whitechapel. Commercial Street is central to the Ripper crimes. Two of the streets in which murders took place, Hanbury Street (Annie Chapman) and Dorset Street (Mary Kelly), ran off it and Gunthorpe Street (Martha Tabram), then George Yard is the next street along.

On the morning of 9 November 1888, the hideously mutilated body of Mary Jane Kelly was found in her room in Miller's Court, a cul-de-sac off Dorset Street. At Mary's inquest on 12 November, a witness named Sarah Lewis spoke of seeing a man standing outside a lodging house in Dorset Street, opposite the entrance to Miller's Court, at about 2.30 a.m. on the 9th. The man was looking up the Court as if waiting for someone to come out. Lewis, and a woman who lived above Kelly, named Elizabeth Prater, both claimed to have heard a cry of 'murder' shortly before 4.00 a.m.

Hours after Lewis gave her inquest testimony, George Hutchinson came forward to say that at about 2.00 a.m. on 9 November, Kelly had approached him in Commerical Street and asked him for sixpence. Being penniless he declined, and watched as she then went off and picked up a well-dressed man, who she took back to Miller's Court. Hutchinson told the police, 'I then went to the Court to see if I could see them but I could not. I stood there for about three quarters of an hour to see if they came out. They did not so I went away.' As far as we know, the police did not ask Sarah Lewis whether Hutchinson was the man she had seen, although it seems highly likely that he was. The fact that he came forward, following the inquest, suggests that he was frightened of being thought of as the murderer and went to the police to clear himself. Certainly, nobody takes all of Hutchinson's statement at face value; the description which he gave of Kelly's client was ridiculously over-elaborated and at the very least greatly exaggerated.

But this has led to the accusation that Hutchinson was not merely frightened of becoming a suspect, but was in fact the Ripper himself, and was looking to throw the police off his scent by portraying himself as an innocent bystander. This theory has gained its share of adherents in recent years. Bob Hinton, who is a very able crime historian, is one; the late Stephen Wright, an American writer, and last year Ben Court and Caroline Ip, the writers of the splendid *Whitechapel* mini-series, are also among them.

Hinton speculates that Hutchinson became obsessed with Mary Kelly and was stalking her. In the convoluted insanity, which grips the mind of the stalker, something, or somebody, has to be responsible for preventing him from being with the object of his desire. In this case, it was the fact of Mary being a prostitute and he blamed this on her sisters-in-trade, whom he slew into perdition. But when she continued to reject him, his love turned to hate and he turned his knife on her.

There is a fact about Kelly's murder, hitherto overlooked, which does make this thesis credible. This type of killer will turn the victim's head away from themselves – cover the face even – so that those dead, accusing eyes cannot appear to be following them, especially when they leave. This happened in the cases of Chapman, Stride and Eddowes. But when we look at the photograph of Mary's remains, her face is turned towards her killer, looking up at him as if she is at long-last treating him with the respect he believes he deserves. What this suggests is that the hatred apparent in this murder was deeply personal.

Now the buts. In the diseased mind of a serial killer, any form of rebuff, no matter how trivial, can have this effect. Moreover, the evidence points to Mary having only returned to prostitution when Joe Barnett moved out at the end of October, i.e. after the other murders. This enormously weakens a hypothesis never strong on hard evidence in the first place. In fact, it only really becomes credible if Mary Kelly was not actually a Ripper victim. In that case, it can be argued that in the stalker's eyes, Barnett had previously been the obstacle to her returning his affections (ironically Barnett himself gains plausibility as Mary's killer if she was not murdered by the Ripper).

It is argued that Hutchinson snugly fits into the FBI's profile. Yes and No. He fits the most basic categories, but these can be applied to literally thousands of men in the East End of that time. But we have no evidence of him being violent, or a danger to women, and after November 1888 he simply fades into obscurity.

But perhaps the most important thing about Aaron Cohen and George Hutchinson is that they surely came from the sort of background from which Jack the Ripper did actually originate. Ordinary and mundane; not rich, powerful or exciting.

Is he in this book? Yes, I believe that he is amongst the ten specific candidates assessed for you by my colleagues. But I will not attempt to prejudice your minds by revealing which one I think he is.

Bibliography

Begg, P., Fido, M. & Skinner, K., *The Jack the Ripper A–Z* (Headline, 2010)

Fairclough, M., *The Ripper and the Royals* (Duckworth, 1991)

Fido, M., *The Crimes, Detection and Death of Jack the Ripper* (Weidenfeld & Nicolson, 1987)

Harris, M., *Jack the Ripper: The Bloody Truth* (Virgin Books, 1987)

Harris, M., *The True Face of Jack the Ripper* (Caxton Editions, 1994)

Harrison, M., *Clarence: Was He Jack the Ripper?* (Drake, 1972)

Hinton, B., *From Hell...The Mystery of Jack the Ripper* (Old Bakehouse Publications, 1998)

Knight, S., *Jack the Ripper, The Final Solution* (Chambers Harrap Publishing, 1976)

Wilding, J., *Jack the Ripper Revealed* (Constable, 1993)

William Beadle is the Chair of The Whitechapel Society and the author of *Jack the Ripper: Anatomy of a Myth* (1995) and *Jack the Ripper Unmasked* (2009). He is also a member of Mensa and several other societies: Dealy Plaza (Kennedy Assassination), Richard III, the Victorian Military Society and the Anglo-Zulu War Society.

Index